MUHAMMAD ALI

Athletes Who Made a Difference

Josh Anderson
illustrated by Kristel Becares

Graphic Universe™ • Minneapolis

Graphic Universe™
An imprint of Lerner Publishing Group, Inc.
241 First Avenue North
Minneapolis, MN 55401 USA

For reading levels and more information, look up this title at www.lernerbooks.com.

Main body text set in CCDaveGibbonsLower
Typeface provided by Comicraft

Photo Acknowledgments
The images in this book are used with the permission of: © Keystone/Stringer/Getty Images, p. 28 (left); © Bettmann/Contributor/Getty Images, p. 28 (right).

Library of Congress Cataloging-in-Publication Data

Names: Anderson, Josh, author. | Becares, Kristel, illustrator.
Title: Muhammad Ali : athletes who made a difference / Josh Anderson ; [illustrated by Kristel Becares].
Description: Minneapolis, MN : Graphic Universe, [2024] | Series: Athletes who made a difference | Includes bibliographical references and index. | Audience: Ages 8–12 years | Audience: Grades 4–6 | Summary: "In graphic nonfiction style, this biography tells the tale of Muhammad Ali's incredible boxing career and lasting civil rights contributions, from the "The Fight of the Century" to becoming a face of the anti-war movement"—Provided by publisher.
Identifiers: LCCN 2023049727 (print) | LCCN 2023049728 (ebook) | ISBN 9781728492964 (library binding) | ISBN 9798765628003 (paperback) | ISBN 9798765631287 (epub)
Subjects: LCSH: Ali, Muhammad, 1942–2016—Juvenile literature. | Boxers (Sports)—United States—Biography—Juvenile literature. | Olympic athletes—United States—Biography—Juvenile literature. | Political activists—United States—Biography—Juvenile literature. | Social reformers—United States—Biography—Juvenile literature.
Classification: LCC GV1132.A4 A53 2024 (print) | LCC GV1132.A4 (ebook) | DDC 796.83092 [B]—dc23/eng/20231213

LC record available at https://lccn.loc.gov/2023049727
LC ebook record available at https://lccn.loc.gov/2023049728

Manufactured in the United States of America
1 – CG – 7/15/24

Table of Contents

CHAPTER 1
SEPARATE AND UNEQUAL

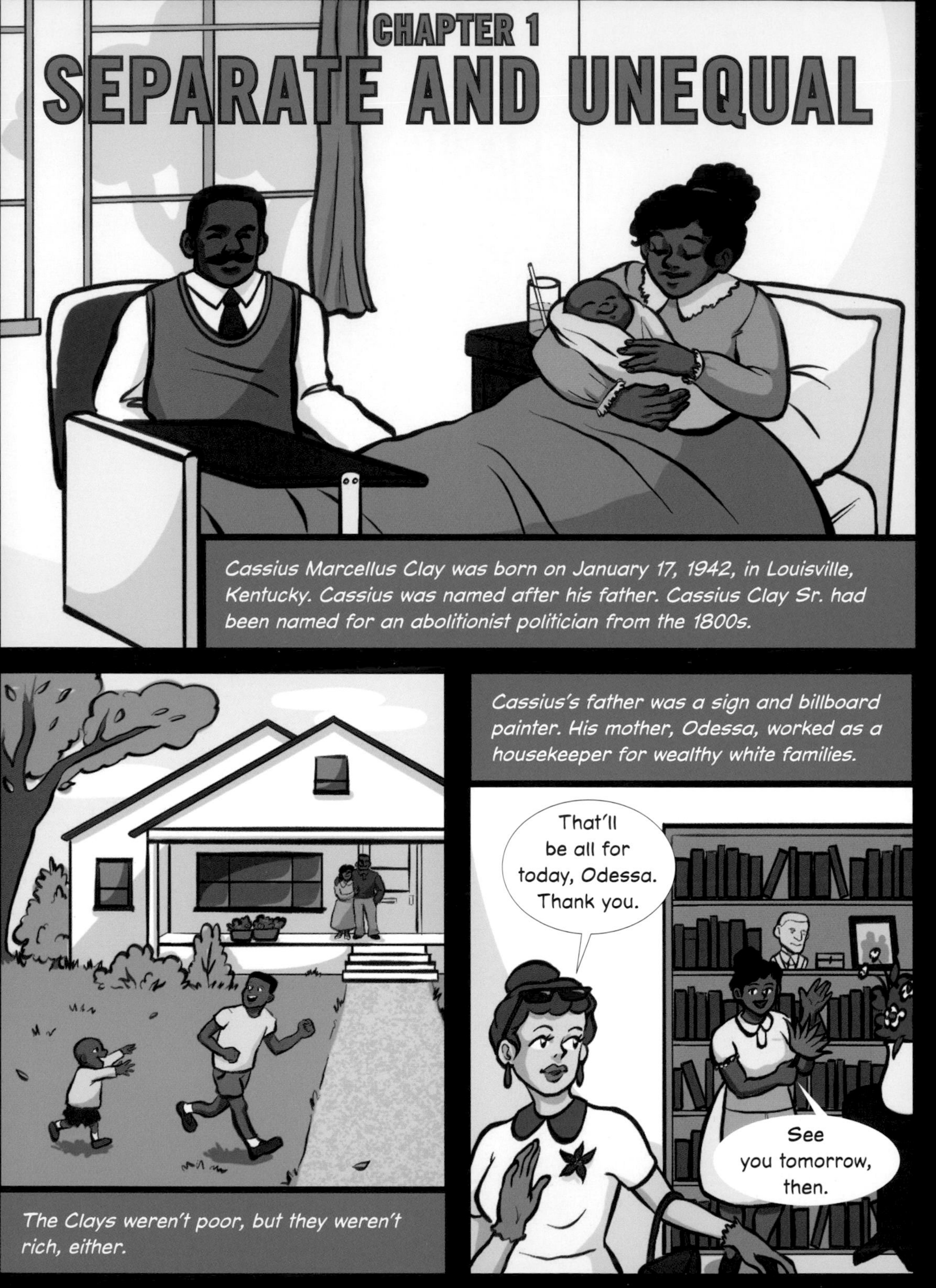

Cassius Marcellus Clay was born on January 17, 1942, in Louisville, Kentucky. Cassius was named after his father. Cassius Clay Sr. had been named for an abolitionist politician from the 1800s.
The Clays weren't poor, but they weren't rich, either.
Cassius's father was a sign and billboard painter. His mother, Odessa, worked as a housekeeper for wealthy white families.
That'll be all for today, Odessa. Thank you.
See you tomorrow, then.

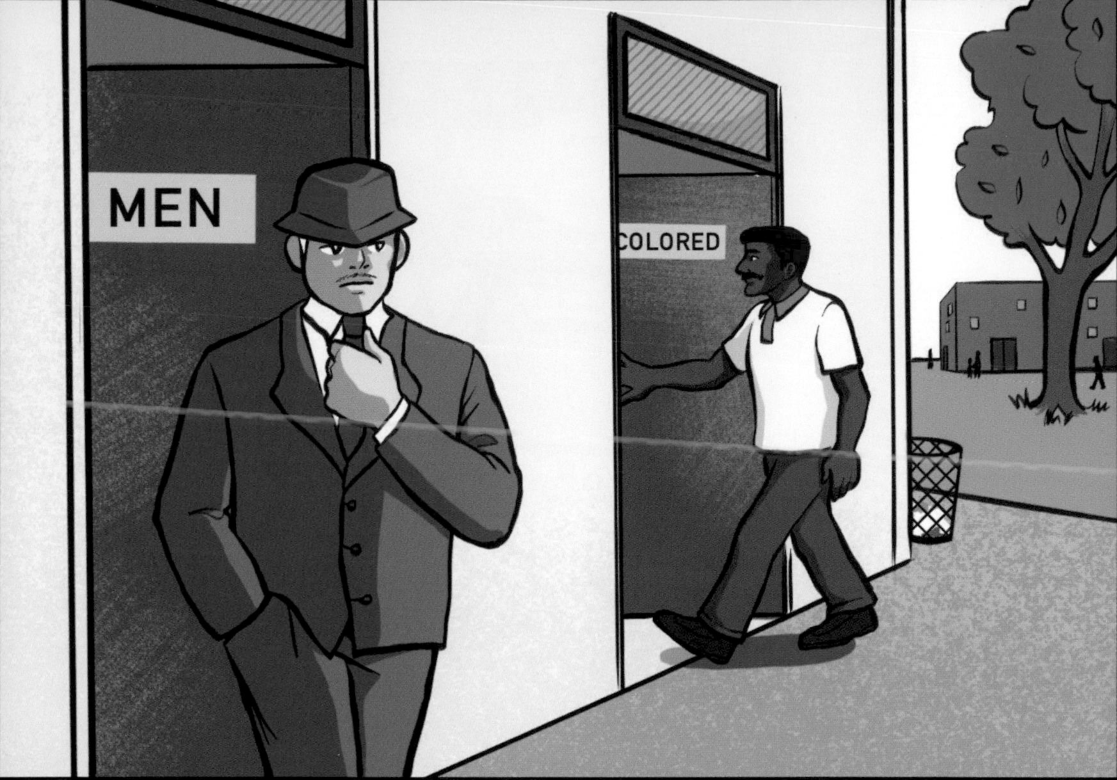
MEN
COLORED

Cassius was born during the time of segregation in the United States. Across the country, Black people were made to live a separate life. They could not attend school with white students. They had to use separate bathrooms. Services like restaurants and public transportation were divided.

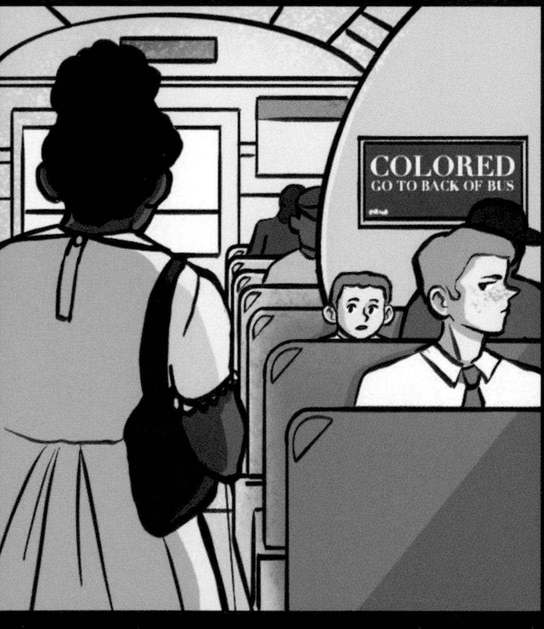
COLORED
GO TO BACK OF BUS

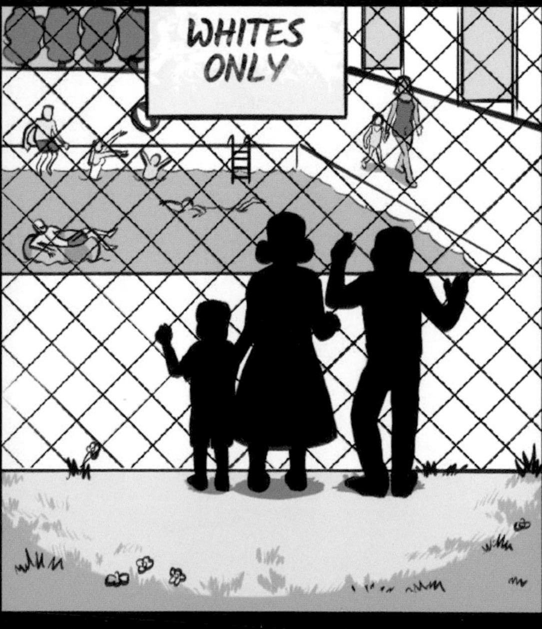
WHITES
ONLY

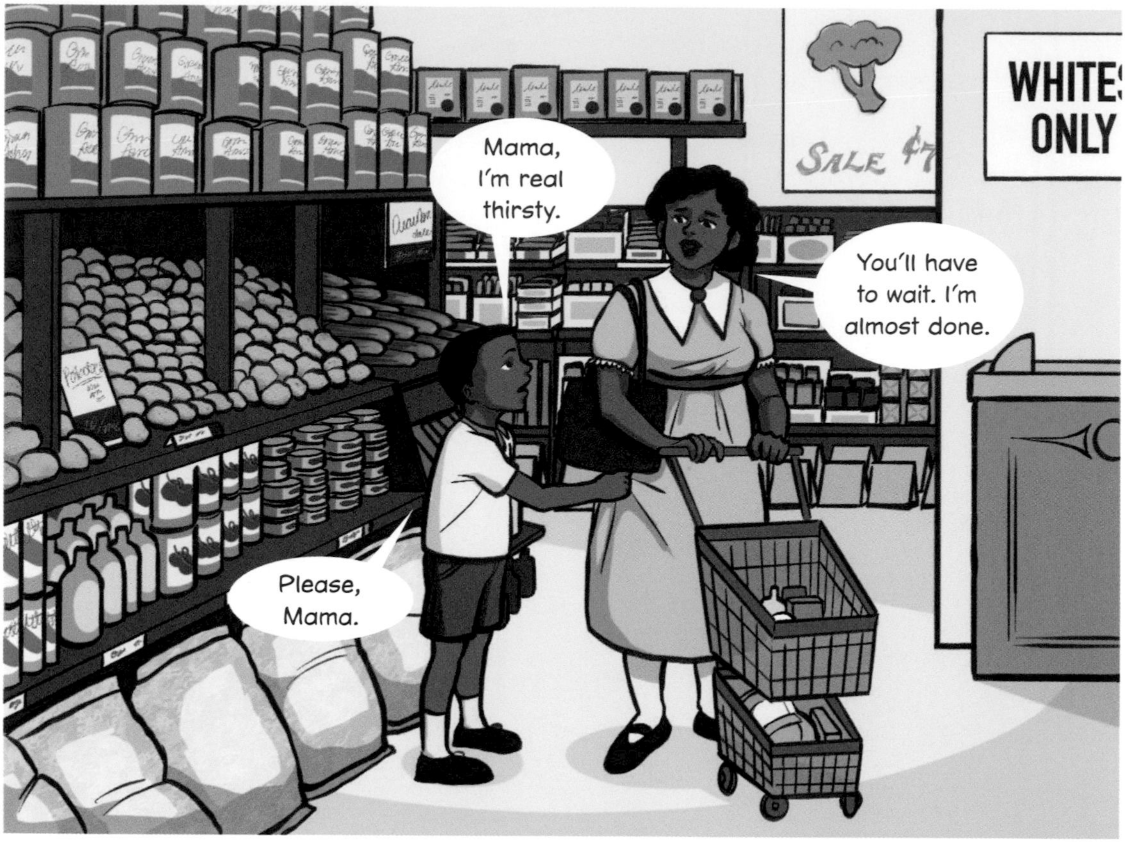
WHITES ONLY
SALE
Mama, I'm real thirsty.
You'll have to wait. I'm almost done.
Please, Mama.

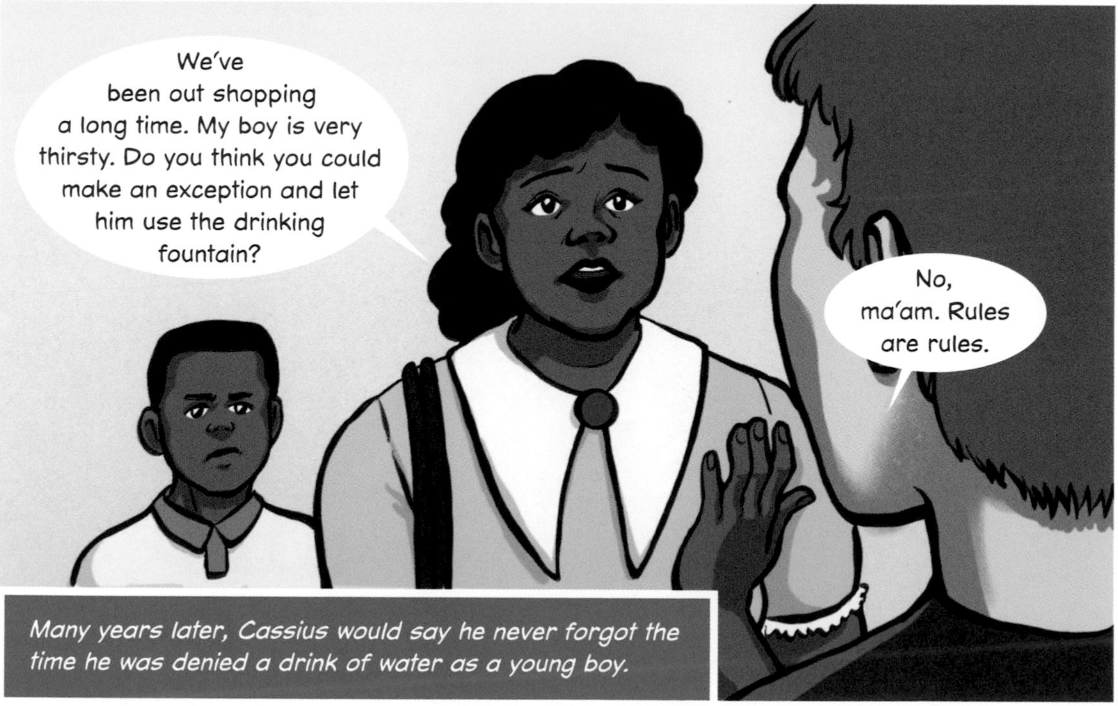
We've been out shopping a long time. My boy is very thirsty. Do you think you could make an exception and let him use the drinking fountain?
No, ma'am. Rules are rules.
Many years later, Cassius would say he never forgot the time he was denied a drink of water as a young boy.

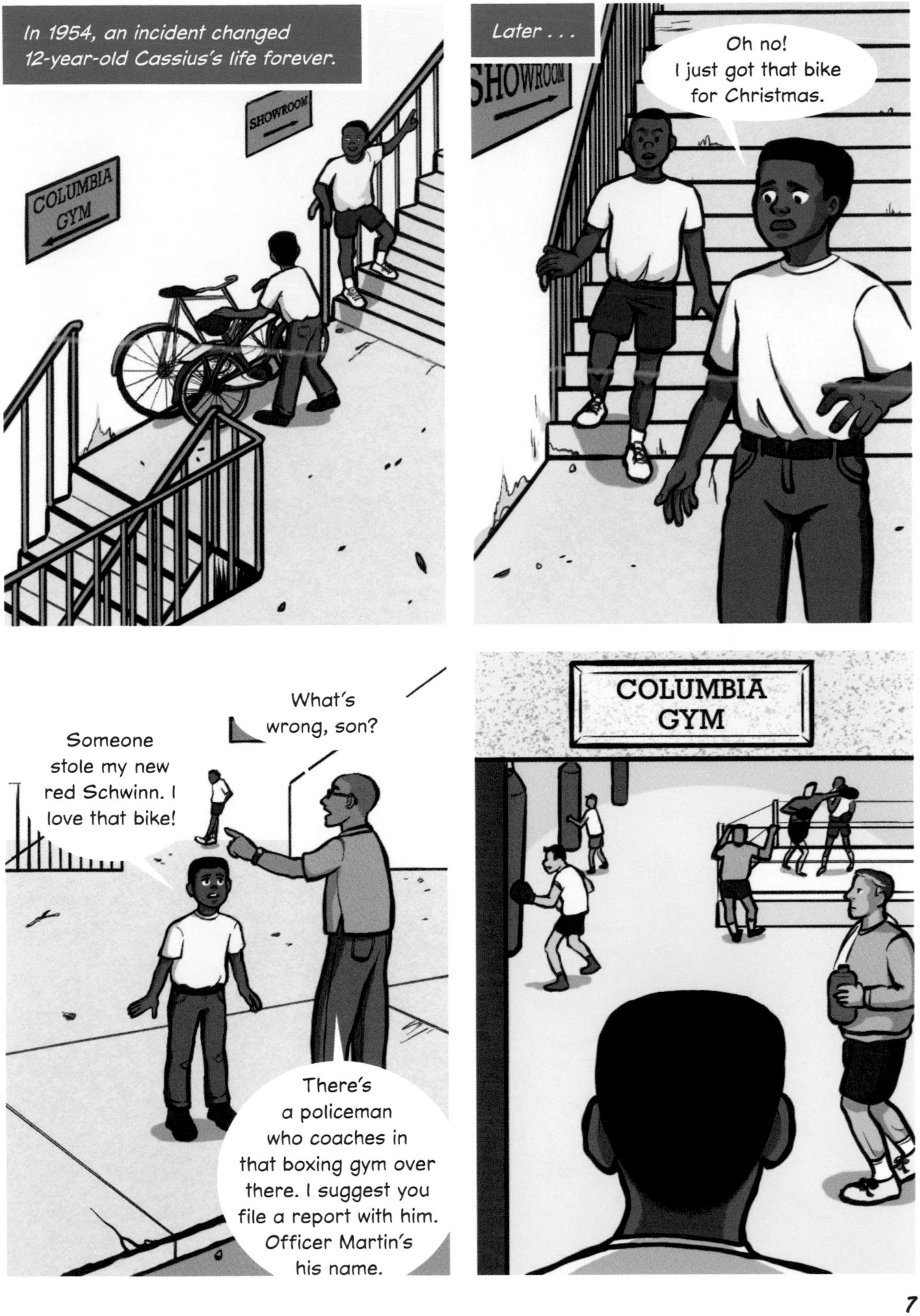
In 1954, an incident changed 12-year-old Cassius's life forever.
SHOWROOM
COLUMBIA GYM
Later . . .
SHOWROOM
Oh no! I just got that bike for Christmas.
What's wrong, son?
Someone stole my new red Schwinn. I love that bike!
There's a policeman who coaches in that boxing gym over there. I suggest you file a report with him. Officer Martin's his name.
COLUMBIA GYM

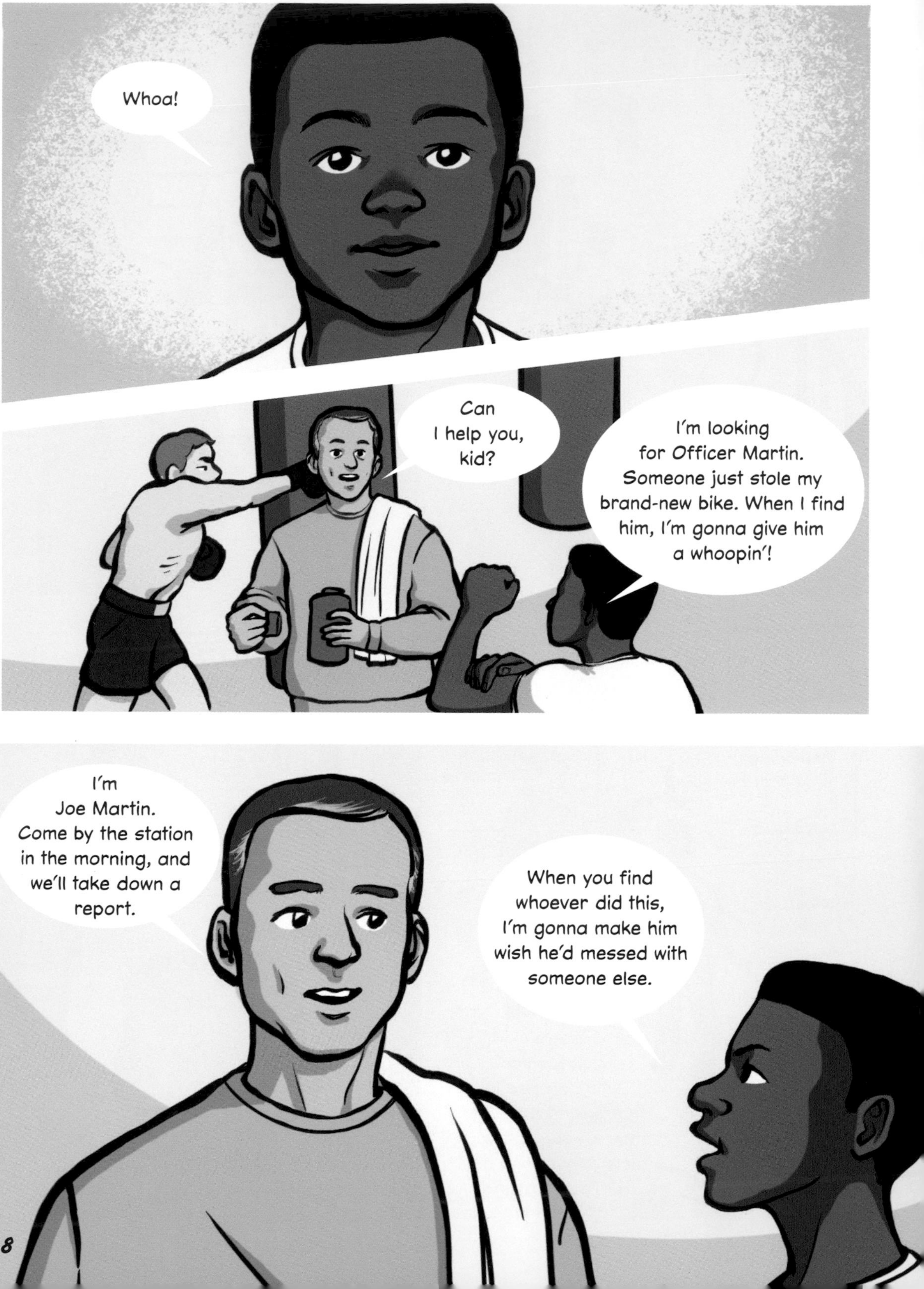
Whoa!
Can I help you, kid?
I'm looking for Officer Martin. Someone just stole my brand-new bike. When I find him, I'm gonna give him a whoopin'!
I'm Joe Martin. Come by the station in the morning, and we'll take down a report.
When you find whoever did this, I'm gonna make him wish he'd messed with someone else.

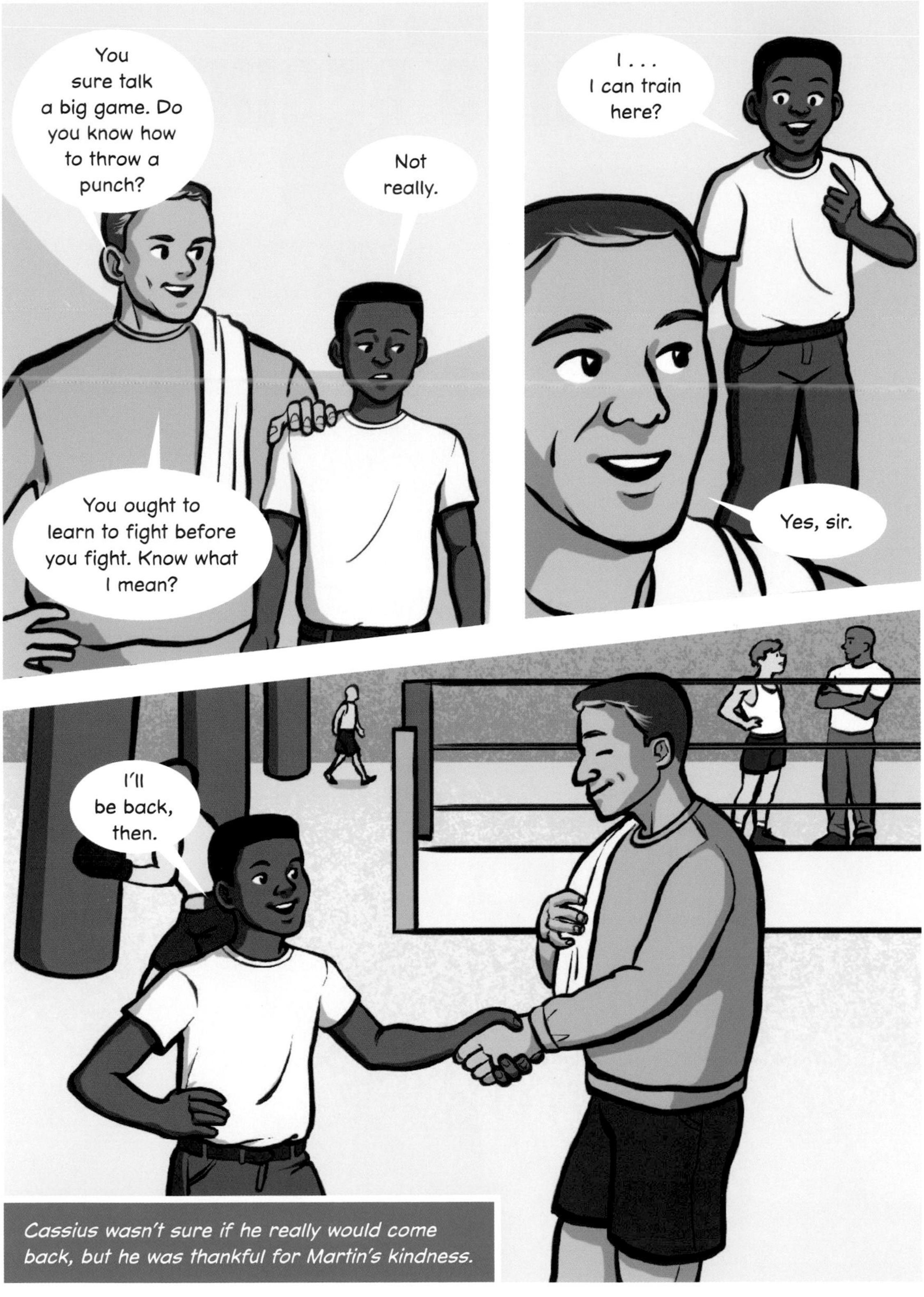
You sure talk a big game. Do you know how to throw a punch?
Not really.
You ought to learn to fight before you fight. Know what I mean?
I . . . I can train here?
Yes, sir.
I'll be back, then.
Cassius wasn't sure if he really would come back, but he was thankful for Martin's kindness.

CHAPTER 2
TRAINING BEGINS

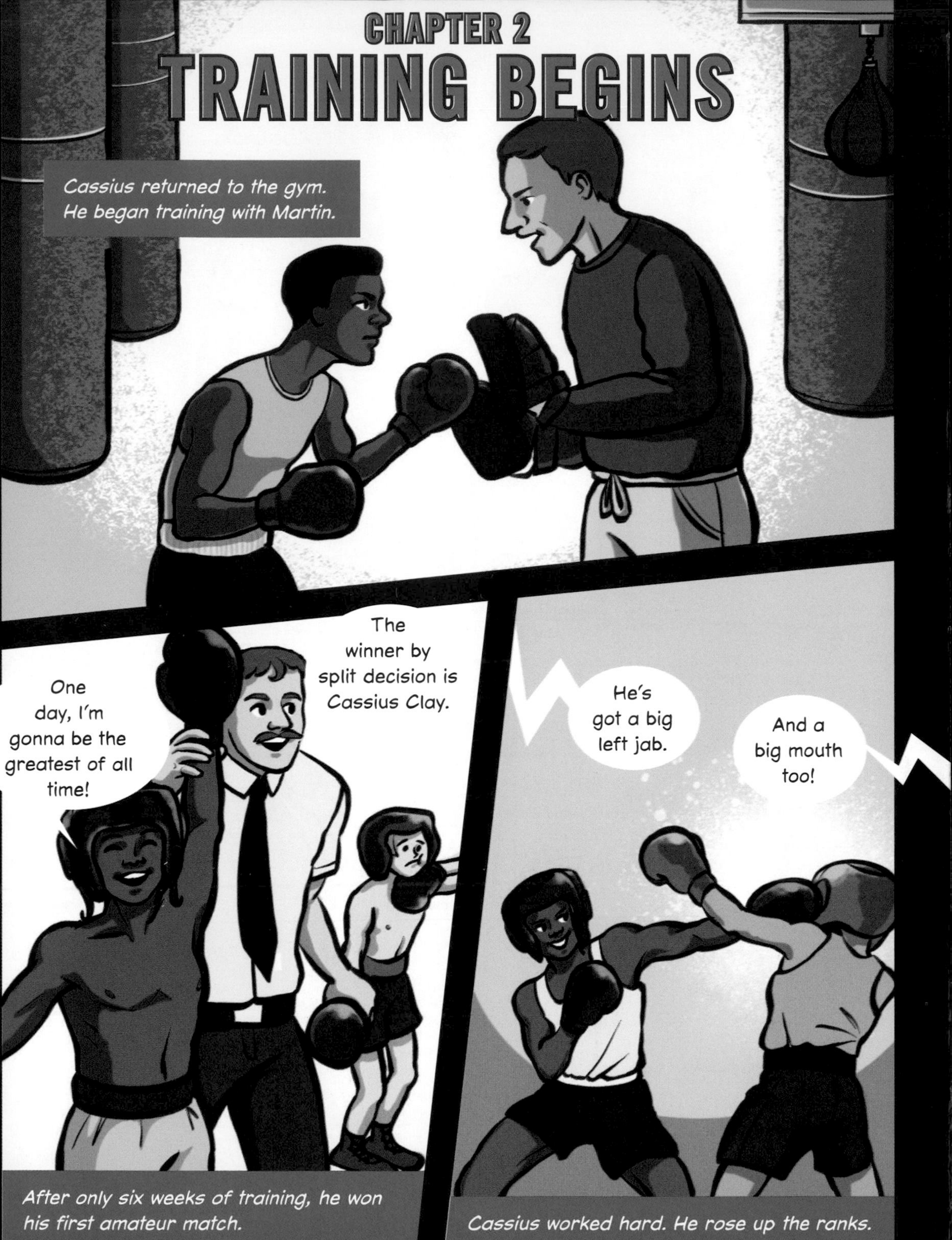
Cassius returned to the gym. He began training with Martin.
One day, I'm gonna be the greatest of all time!
The winner by split decision is Cassius Clay.
After only six weeks of training, he won his first amateur match.
He's got a big left jab.
And a big mouth too!
Cassius worked hard. He rose up the ranks.

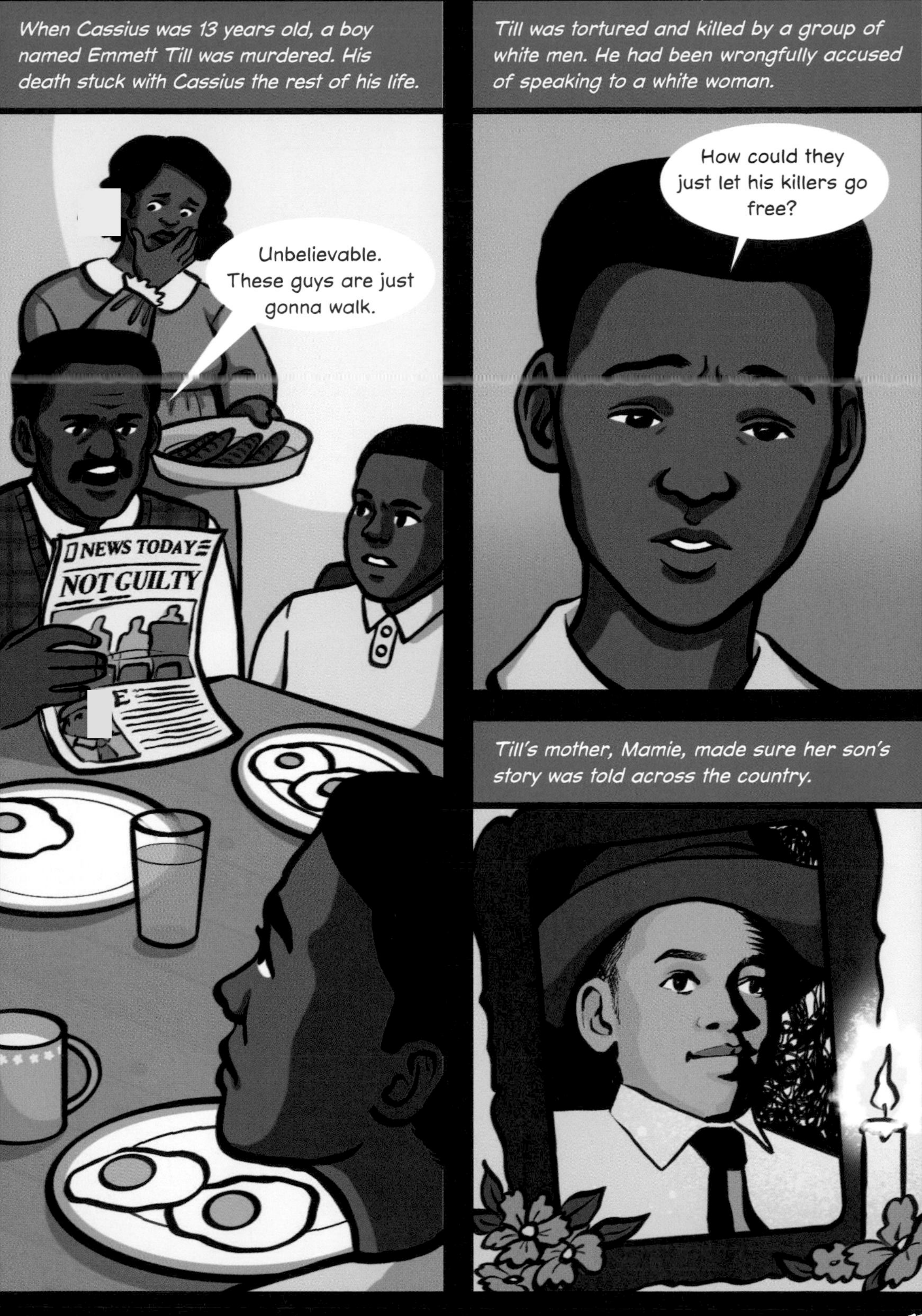
When Cassius was 13 years old, a boy named Emmett Till was murdered. His death stuck with Cassius the rest of his life.
Unbelievable. These guys are just gonna walk.
NEWS TODAY
NOT GUILTY
Till was tortured and killed by a group of white men. He had been wrongfully accused of speaking to a white woman.
How could they just let his killers go free?
Till's mother, Mamie, made sure her son's story was told across the country.

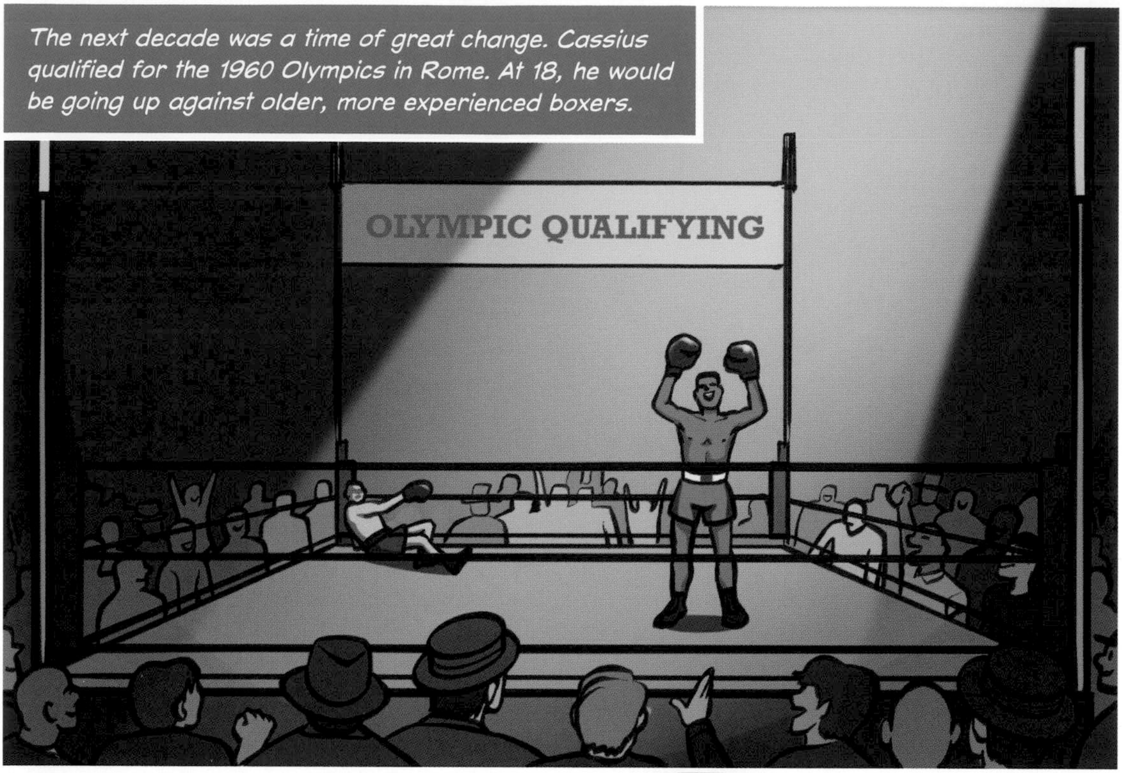
The next decade was a time of great change. Cassius qualified for the 1960 Olympics in Rome. At 18, he would be going up against older, more experienced boxers.
OLYMPIC QUALIFYING

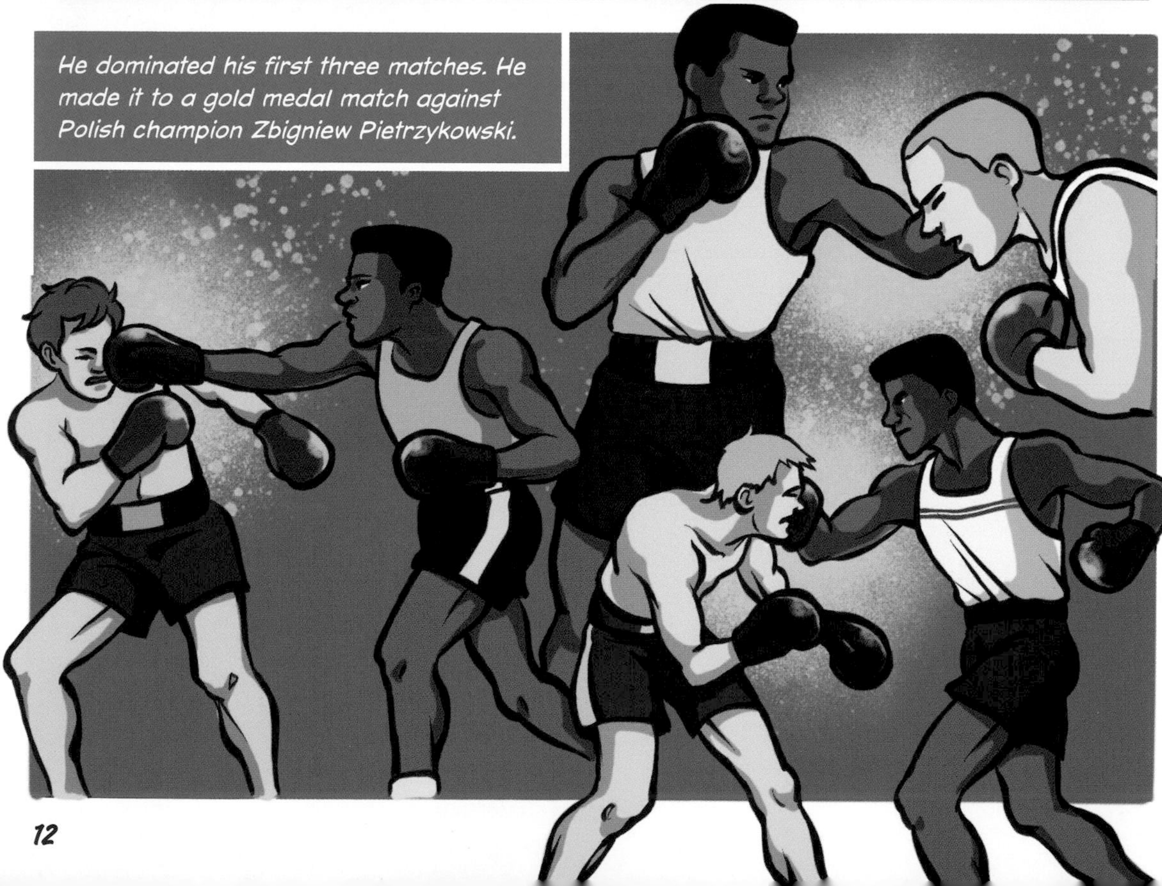
He dominated his first three matches. He made it to a gold medal match against Polish champion Zbigniew Pietrzykowski.

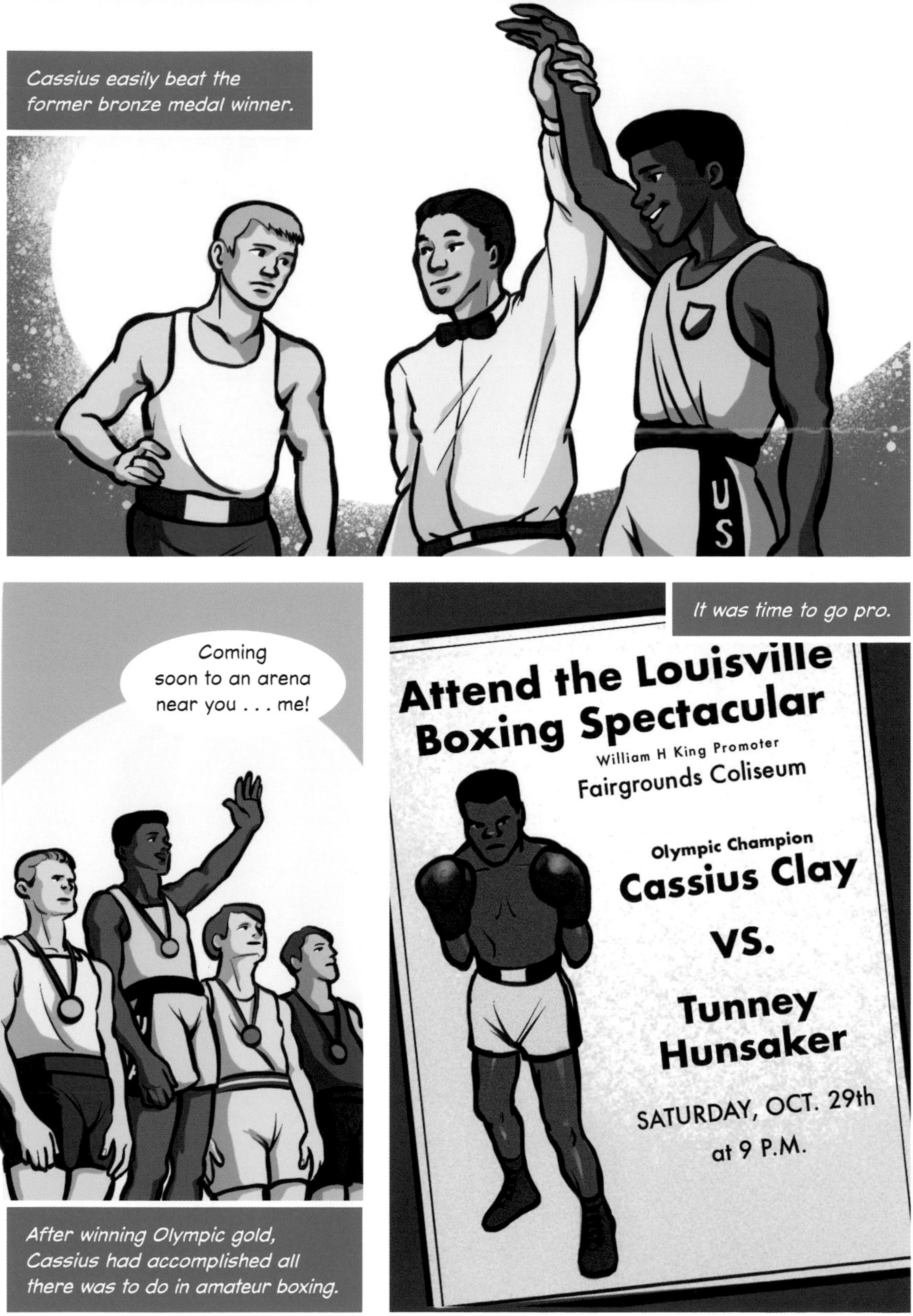
Cassius easily beat the former bronze medal winner.
US
Coming soon to an arena near you . . . me!
After winning Olympic gold, Cassius had accomplished all there was to do in amateur boxing.
It was time to go pro.
Attend the Louisville Boxing Spectacular
William H King Promoter
Fairgrounds Coliseum
Olympic Champion
Cassius Clay
VS.
Tunney Hunsaker
SATURDAY, OCT. 29th
at 9 P.M.

CHAPTER 3
ENTER: CASSIUS CLAY

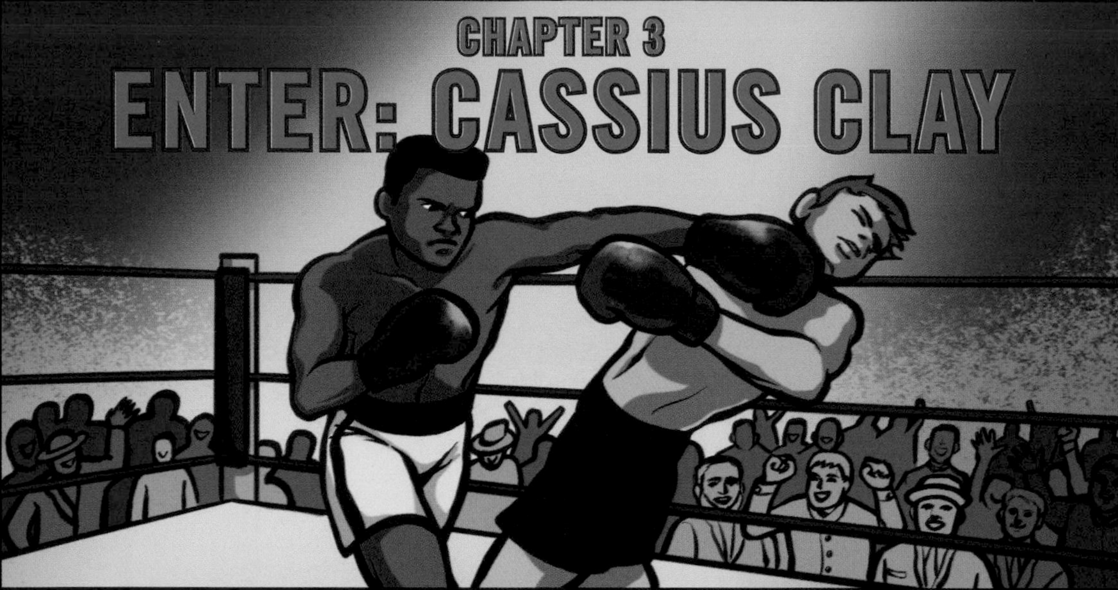

From late 1960 through the end of 1963, Cassius compiled a record of 19 wins and no losses. He defeated tougher and tougher opponents. One was former light-heavyweight champion Archie Moore. He was becoming a symbol of greatness.

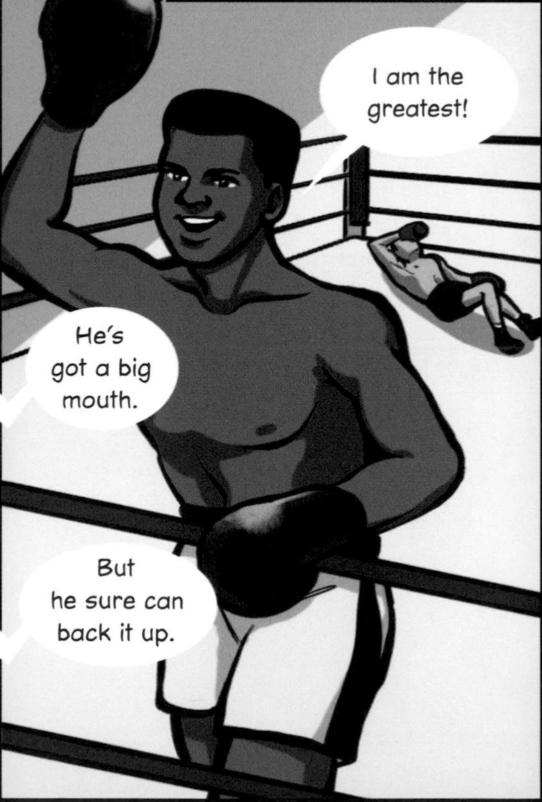
I am the greatest!
He's got a big mouth.
But he sure can back it up.

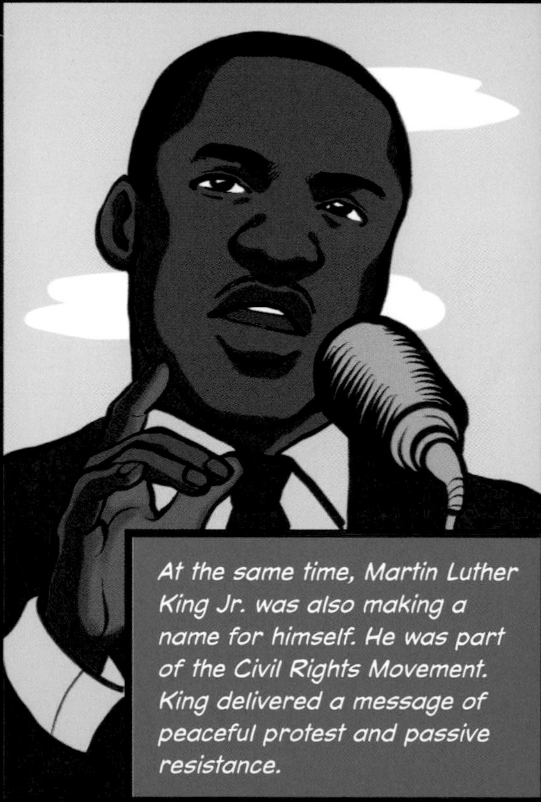
At the same time, Martin Luther King Jr. was also making a name for himself. He was part of the Civil Rights Movement. King delivered a message of peaceful protest and passive resistance.

The Nation of Islam believed in civil rights too. But this group focused on Black unity and defending Black communities. In 1961, Cassius began attending Nation of Islam meetings.

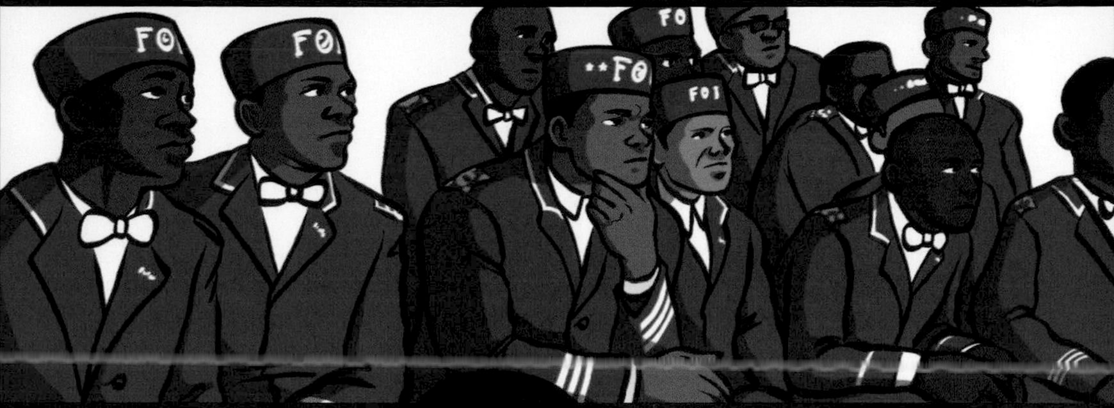
FOI

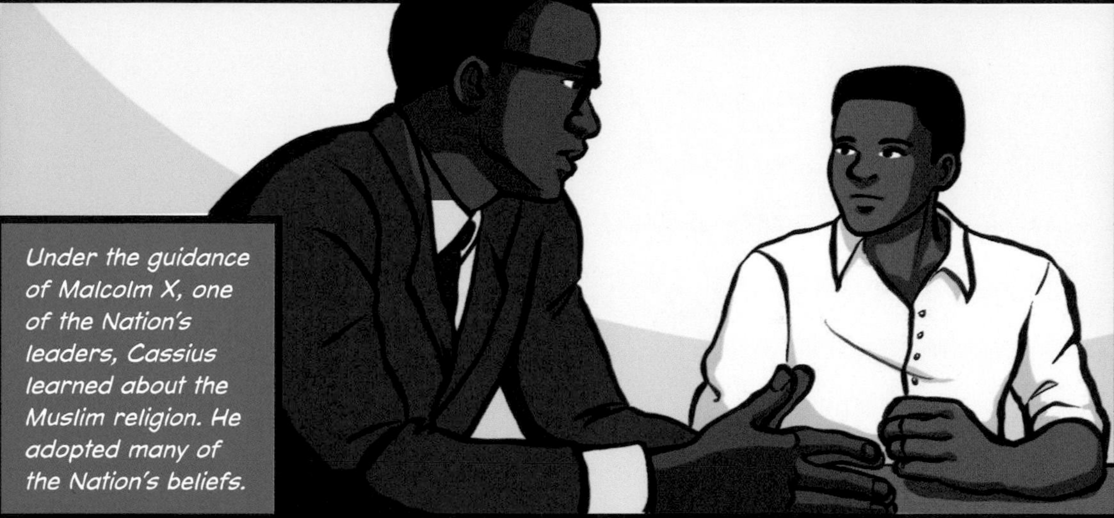
Under the guidance of Malcolm X, one of the Nation's leaders, Cassius learned about the Muslim religion. He adopted many of the Nation's beliefs.

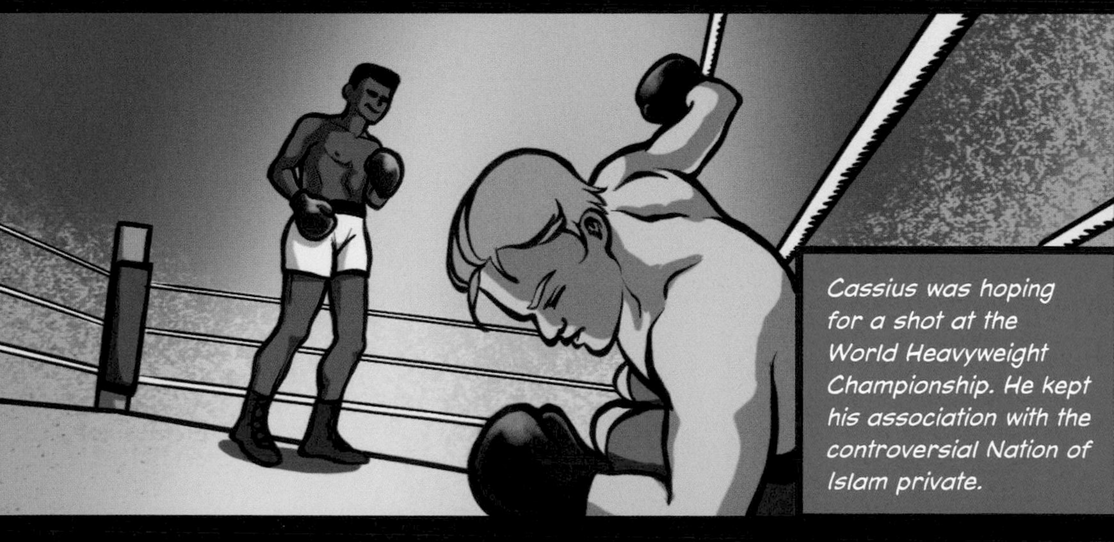
Cassius was hoping for a shot at the World Heavyweight Championship. He kept his association with the controversial Nation of Islam private.

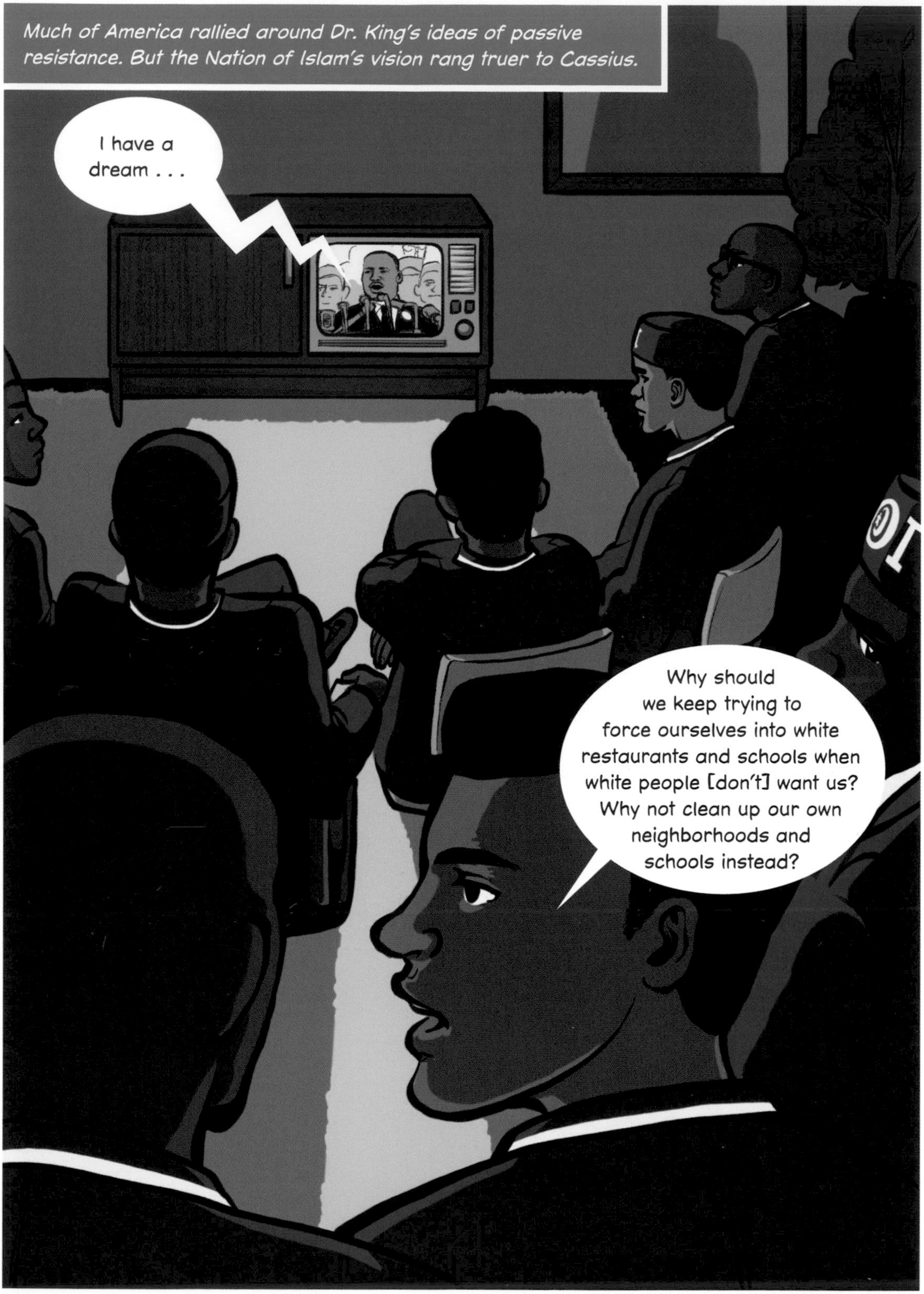
Much of America rallied around Dr. King's ideas of passive resistance. But the Nation of Islam's vision rang truer to Cassius.
I have a dream . . .
Why should we keep trying to force ourselves into white restaurants and schools when white people [don't] want us? Why not clean up our own neighborhoods and schools instead?

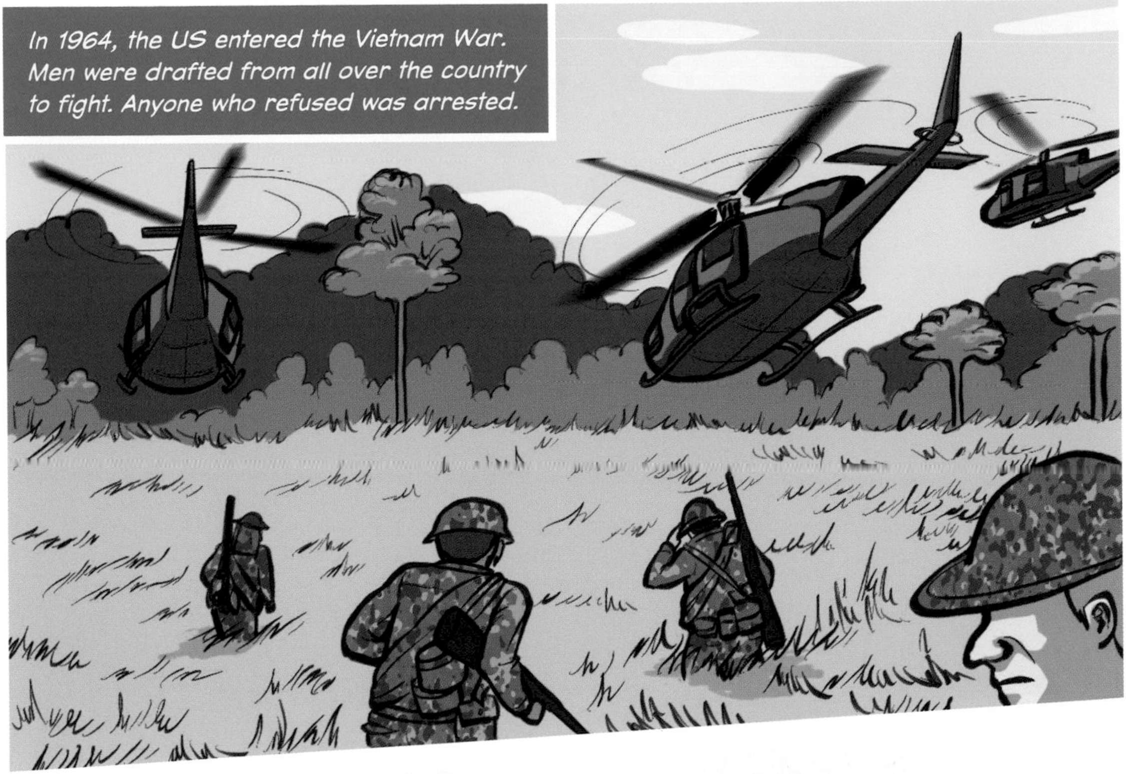
In 1964, the US entered the Vietnam War. Men were drafted from all over the country to fight. Anyone who refused was arrested.

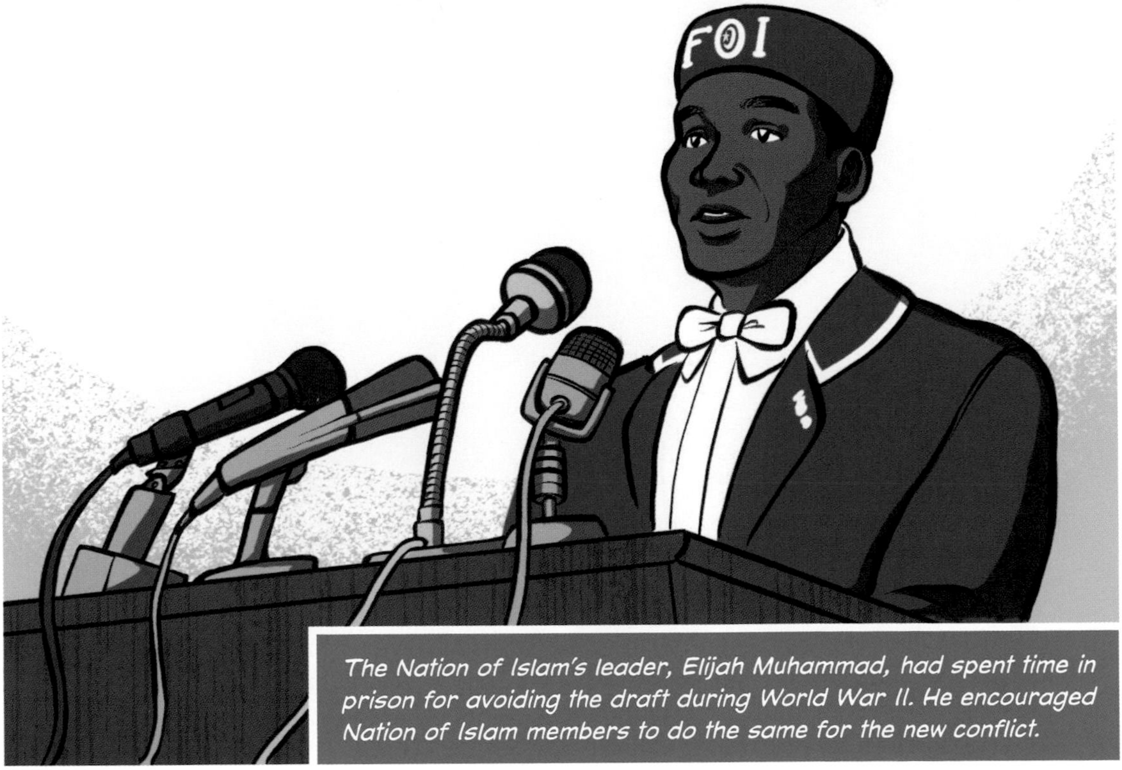
FOI
The Nation of Islam's leader, Elijah Muhammad, had spent time in prison for avoiding the draft during World War II. He encouraged Nation of Islam members to do the same for the new conflict.

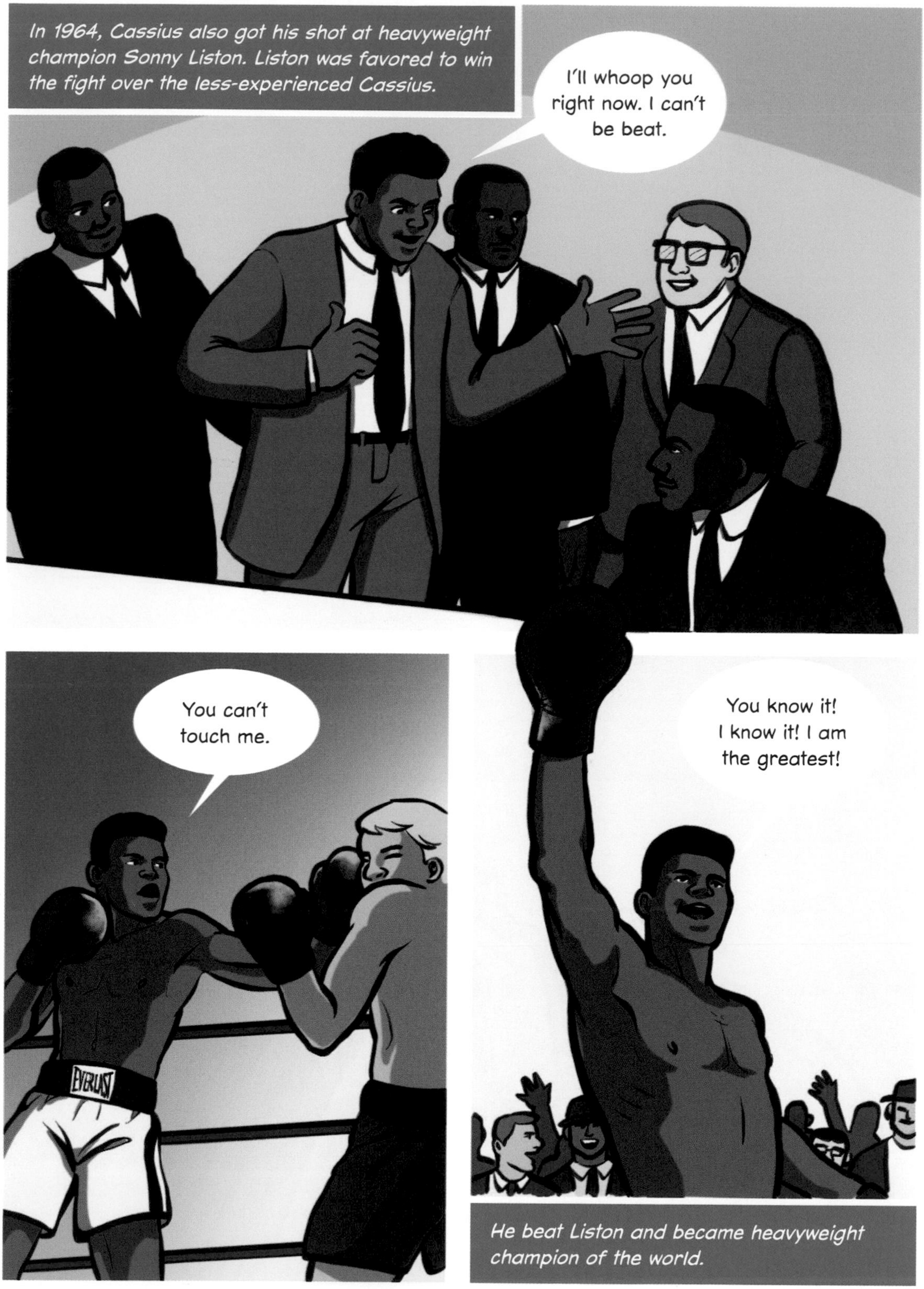
In 1964, Cassius also got his shot at heavyweight champion Sonny Liston. Liston was favored to win the fight over the less-experienced Cassius.
I'll whoop you right now. I can't be beat.
You can't touch me.
EVERLAST
You know it! I know it! I am the greatest!
He beat Liston and became heavyweight champion of the world.

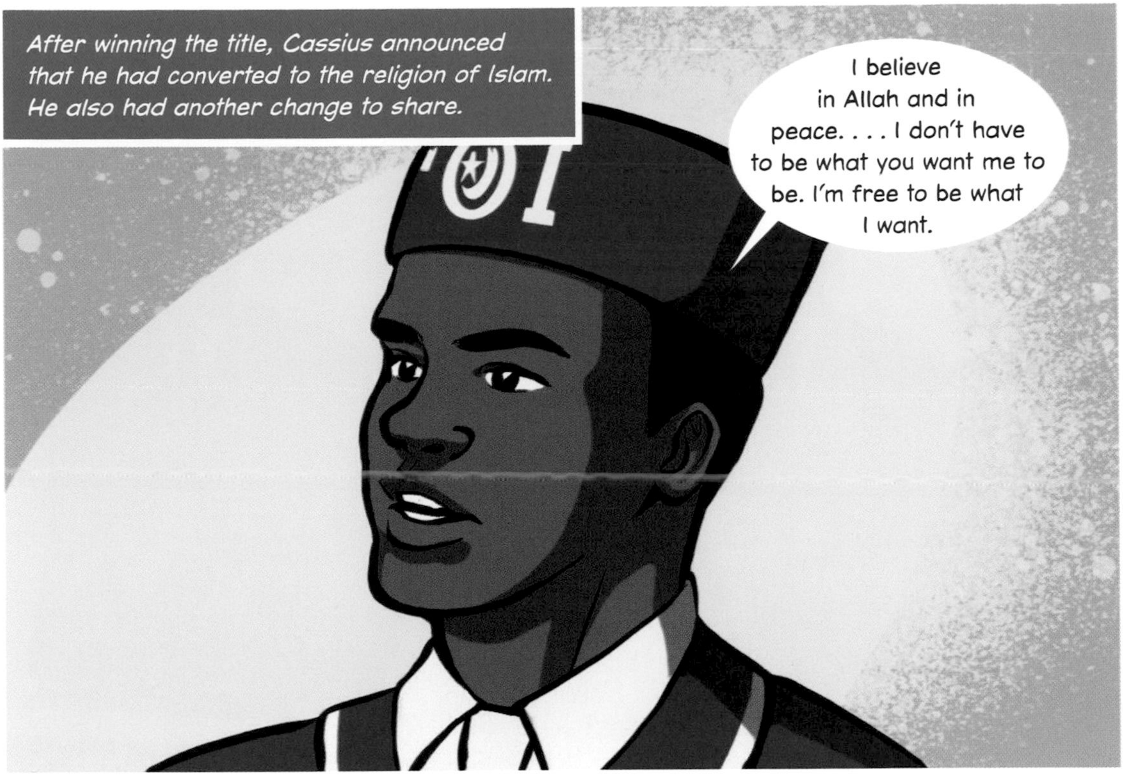
After winning the title, Cassius announced that he had converted to the religion of Islam. He also had another change to share.
I believe in Allah and in peace. . . . I don't have to be what you want me to be. I'm free to be what I want.

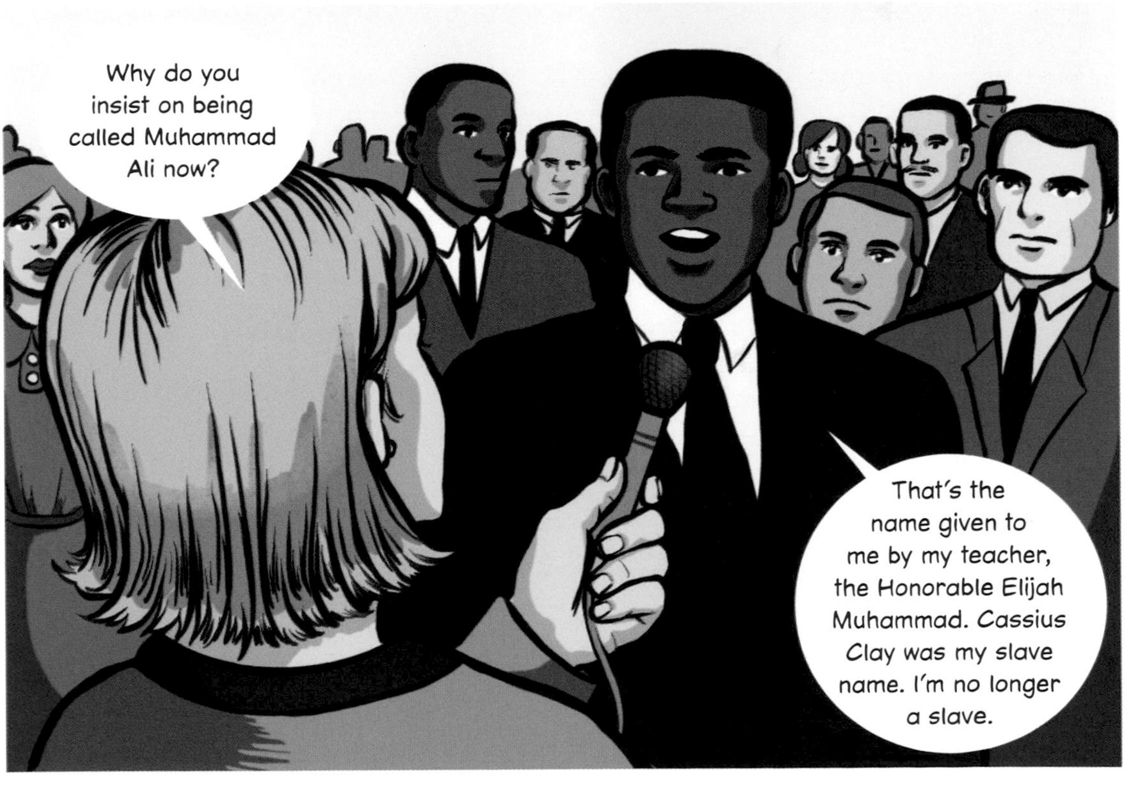
Why do you insist on being called Muhammad Ali now?
That's the name given to me by my teacher, the Honorable Elijah Muhammad. Cassius Clay was my slave name. I'm no longer a slave.

Muhammad paid a price for speaking out. The World Boxing Association took away one of his championship belts. Many people around the country stopped cheering for him.

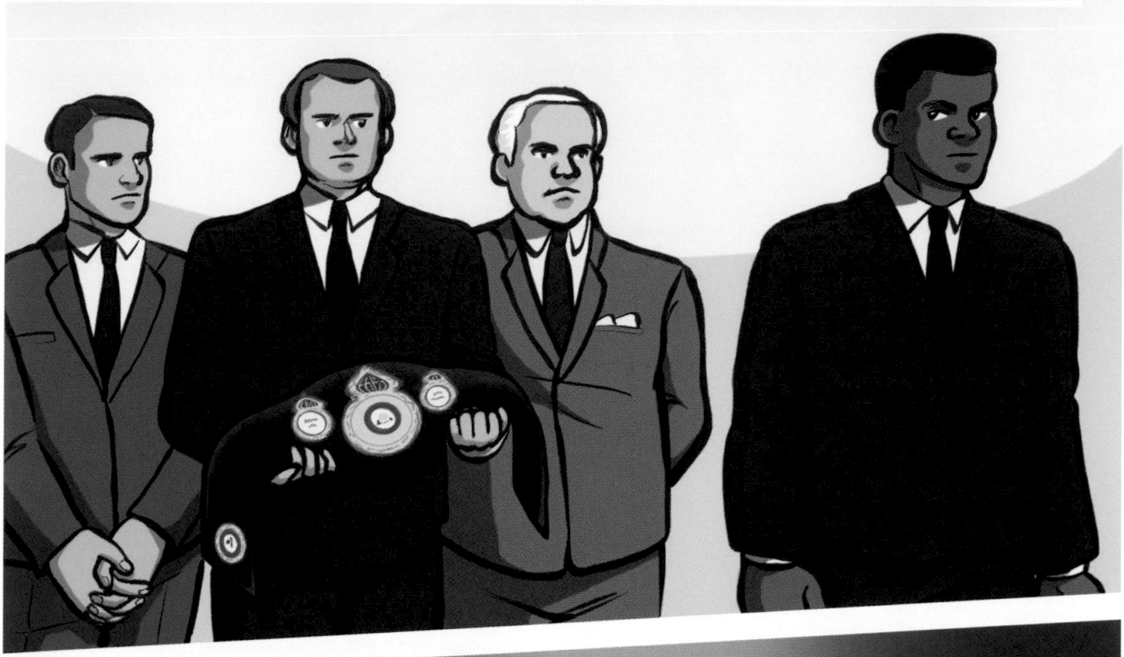

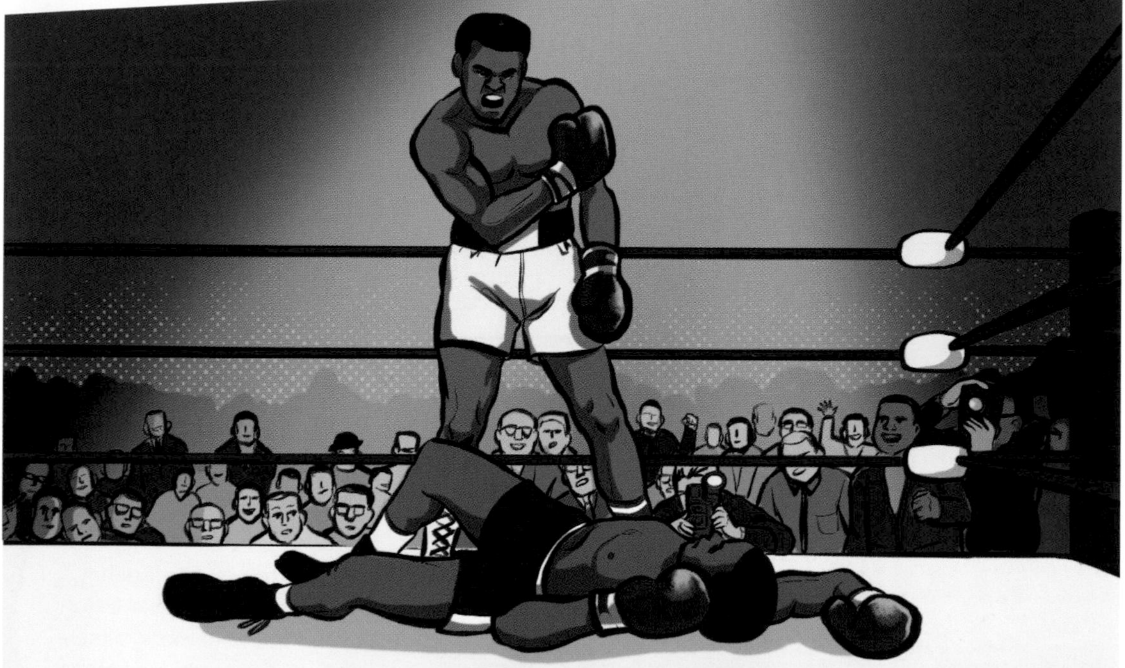

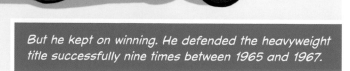

But he kept on winning. He defended the heavyweight title successfully nine times between 1965 and 1967.

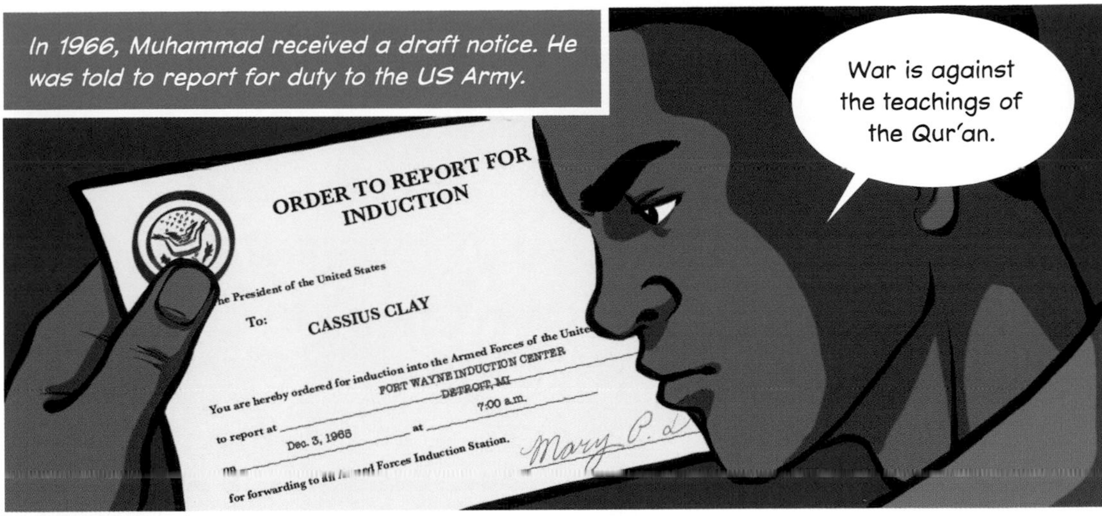
In 1966, Muhammad received a draft notice. He was told to report for duty to the US Army.
War is against the teachings of the Qur'an.
ORDER TO REPORT FOR INDUCTION
To: CASSIUS CLAY
FORT WAYNE INDUCTION CENTER
7:00 a.m.

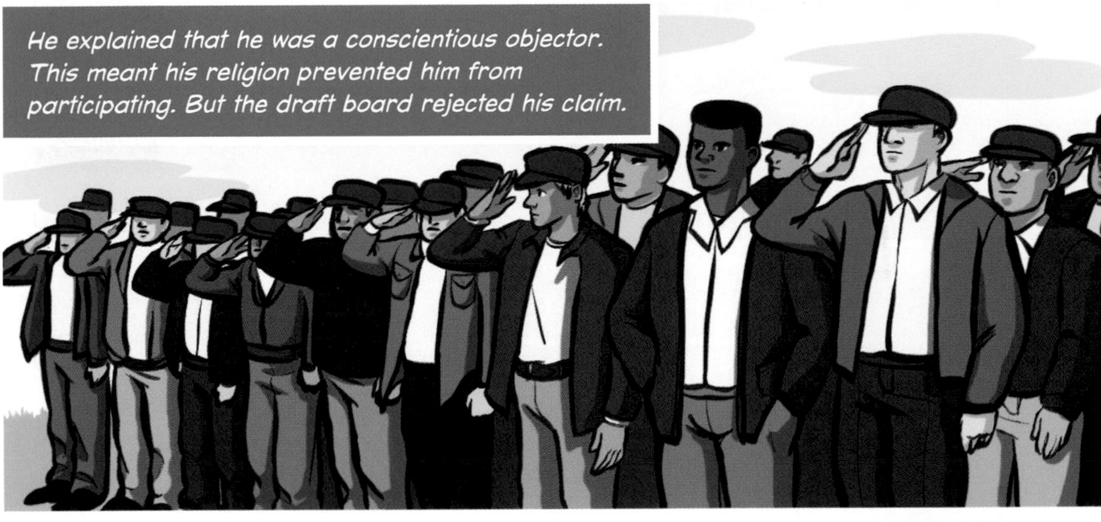
He explained that he was a conscientious objector. This meant his religion prevented him from participating. But the draft board rejected his claim.

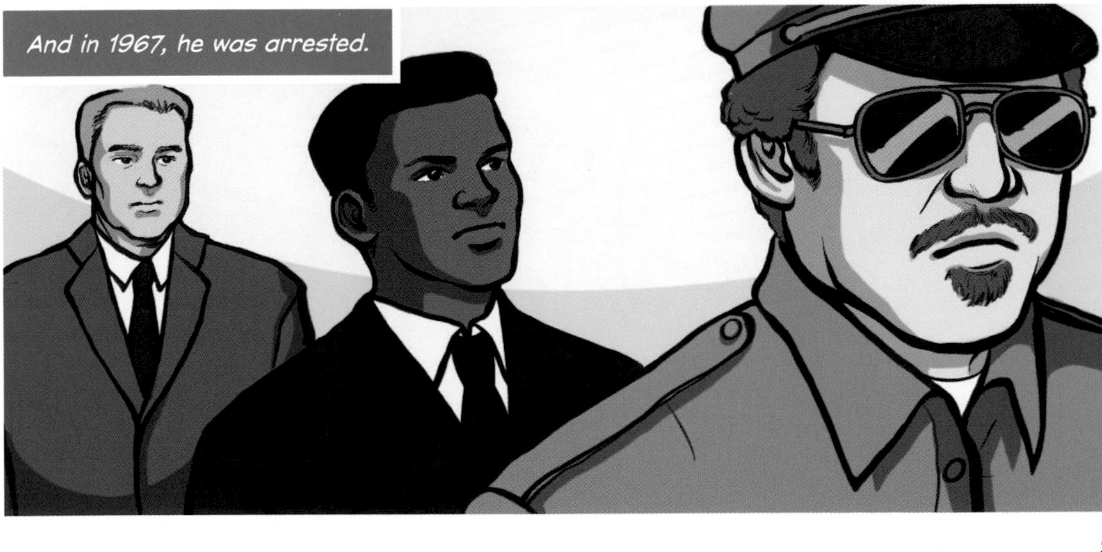
And in 1967, he was arrested.

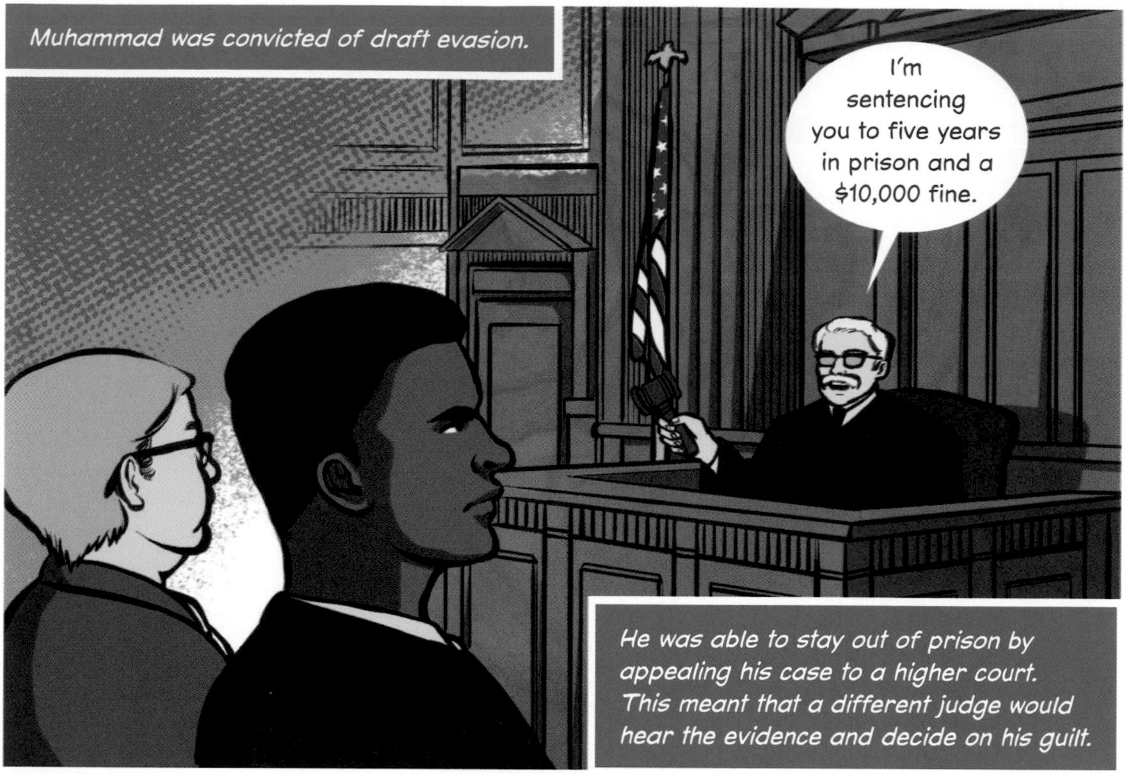
Muhammad was convicted of draft evasion.
I'm sentencing you to five years in prison and a $10,000 fine.
He was able to stay out of prison by appealing his case to a higher court. This meant that a different judge would hear the evidence and decide on his guilt.

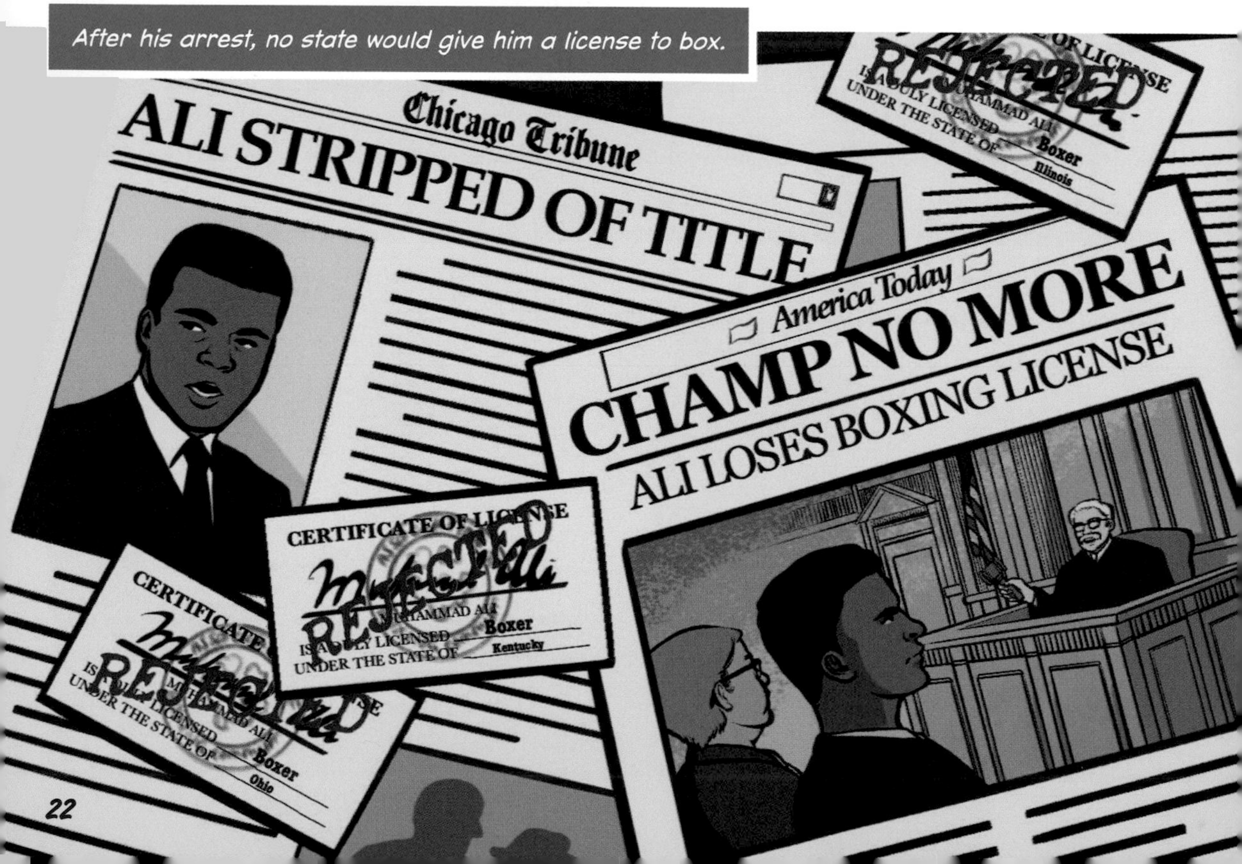
After his arrest, no state would give him a license to box.
Chicago Tribune
ALI STRIPPED OF TITLE
America Today
CHAMP NO MORE
ALI LOSES BOXING LICENSE
REJECTED
UNDER THE STATE OF
Boxer
Illinois
CERTIFICATE OF LICENSE
REJECTED
MUHAMMAD ALI
Boxer
UNDER THE STATE OF
Kentucky
CERTIFICATE
REJECTED
UNDER THE STATE OF
Boxer
Ohio

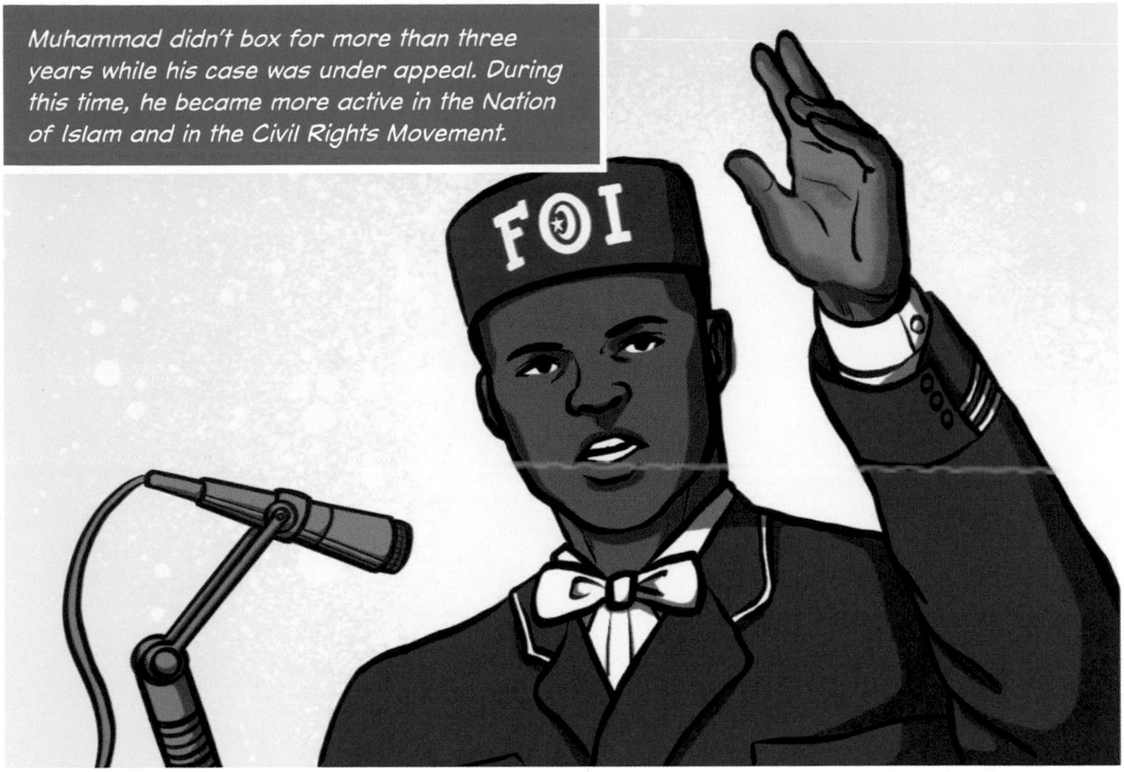
Muhammad didn't box for more than three years while his case was under appeal. During this time, he became more active in the Nation of Islam and in the Civil Rights Movement.
FOI

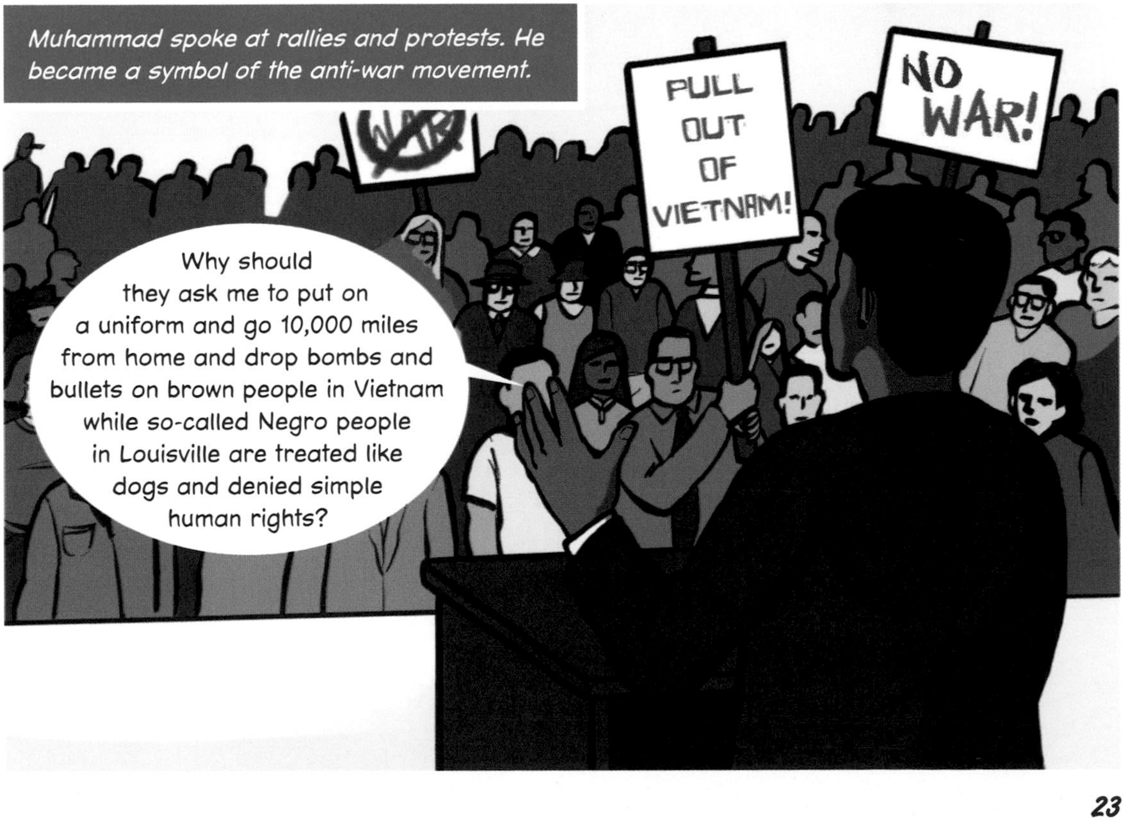
Muhammad spoke at rallies and protests. He became a symbol of the anti-war movement.
PULL OUT OF VIETNAM!
NO WAR!
Why should they ask me to put on a uniform and go 10,000 miles from home and drop bombs and bullets on brown people in Vietnam while so-called Negro people in Louisville are treated like dogs and denied simple human rights?

CHAPTER 4
PUNCHING UP

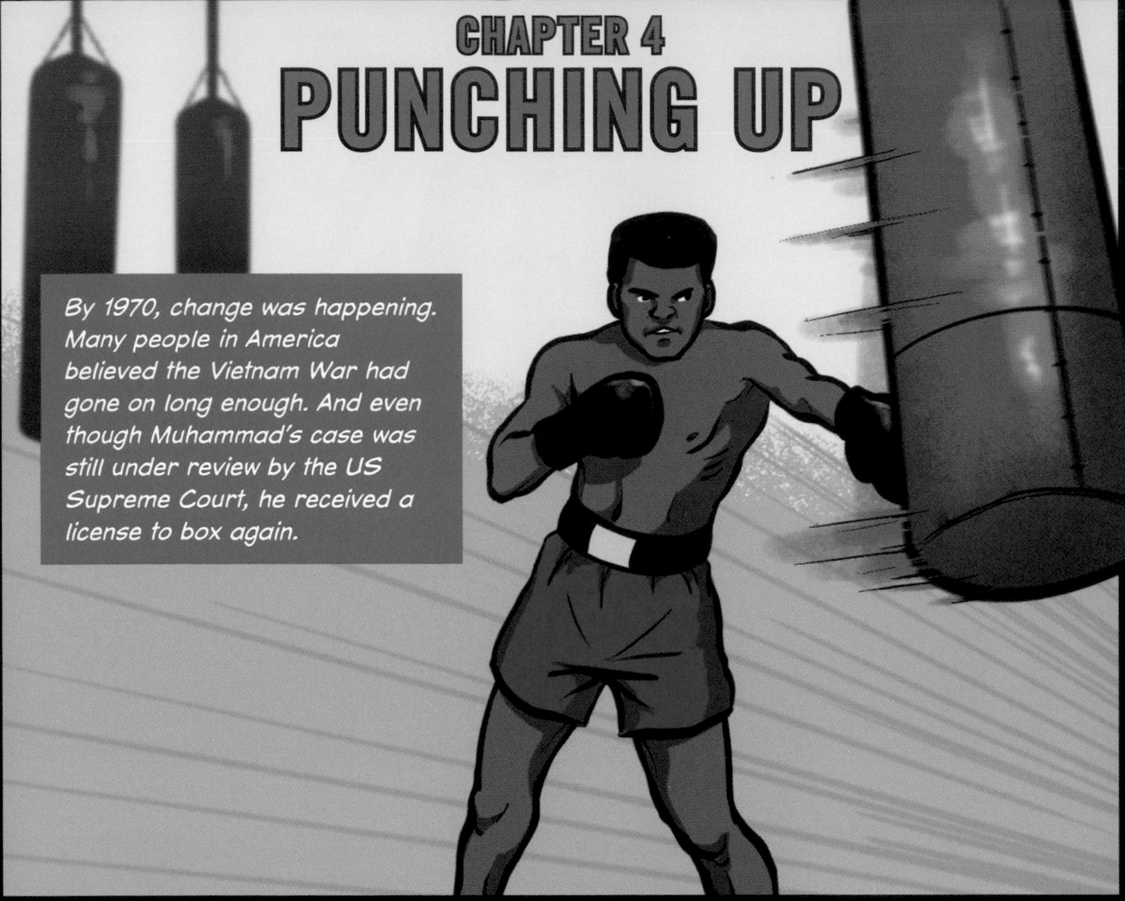
By 1970, change was happening. Many people in America believed the Vietnam War had gone on long enough. And even though Muhammad's case was still under review by the US Supreme Court, he received a license to box again.

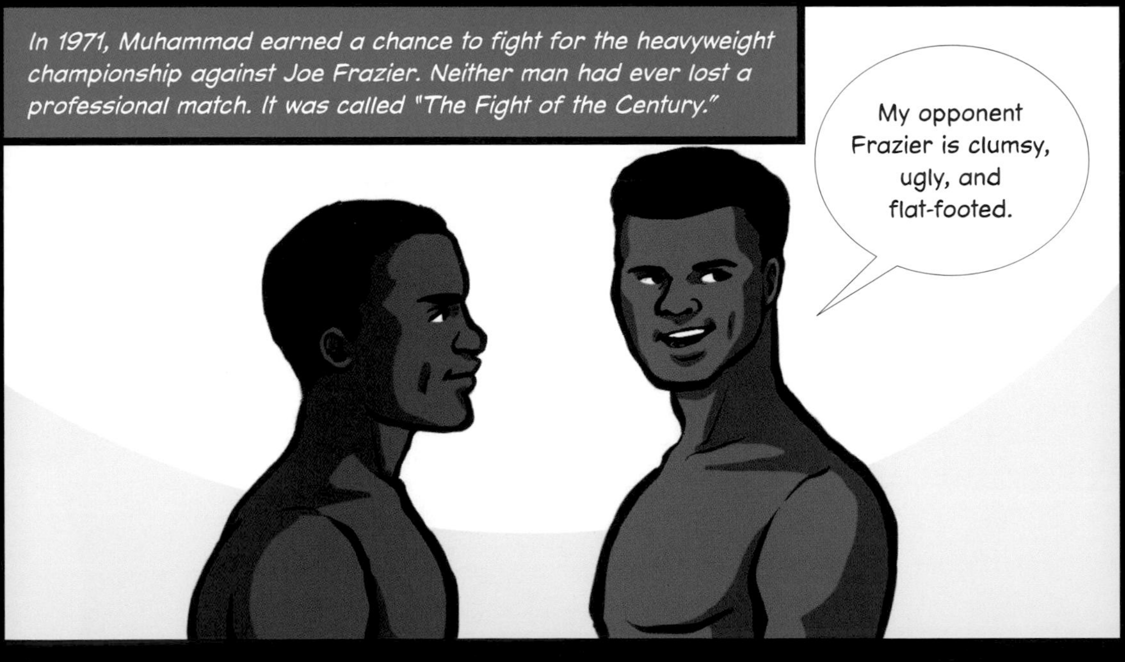
In 1971, Muhammad earned a chance to fight for the heavyweight championship against Joe Frazier. Neither man had ever lost a professional match. It was called "The Fight of the Century."
My opponent Frazier is clumsy, ugly, and flat-footed.

For 15 rounds, the former champion battled the current champion.

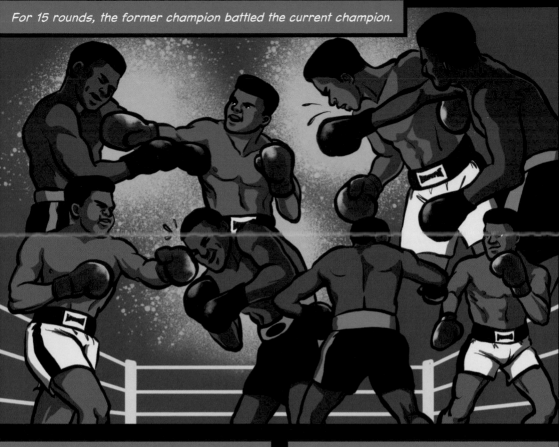

At the end of the match, Muhammad lost on the judge's scorecards for the first time in his career.

But a different kind of victory was right around the corner. In June of 1971, the US Supreme Court overturned his conviction of draft evasion. He'd lost nearly four years of his career. But he was finally a free man.

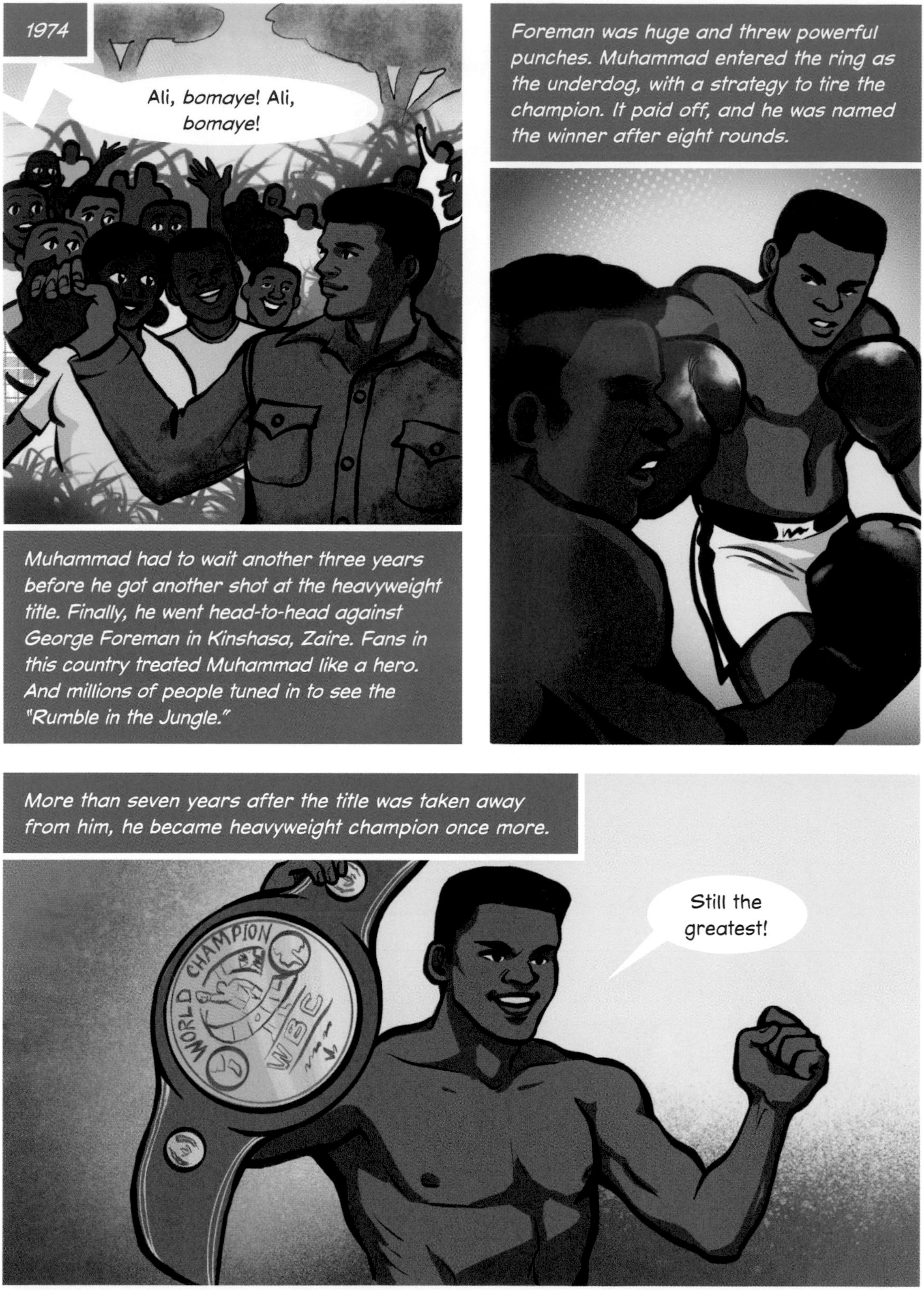
1974
Ali, *bomaye*! Ali, *bomaye*!
Muhammad had to wait another three years before he got another shot at the heavyweight title. Finally, he went head-to-head against George Foreman in Kinshasa, Zaire. Fans in this country treated Muhammad like a hero. And millions of people tuned in to see the "Rumble in the Jungle."
Foreman was huge and threw powerful punches. Muhammad entered the ring as the underdog, with a strategy to tire the champion. It paid off, and he was named the winner after eight rounds.
More than seven years after the title was taken away from him, he became heavyweight champion once more.
WORLD CHAMPION
WBC
Still the greatest!

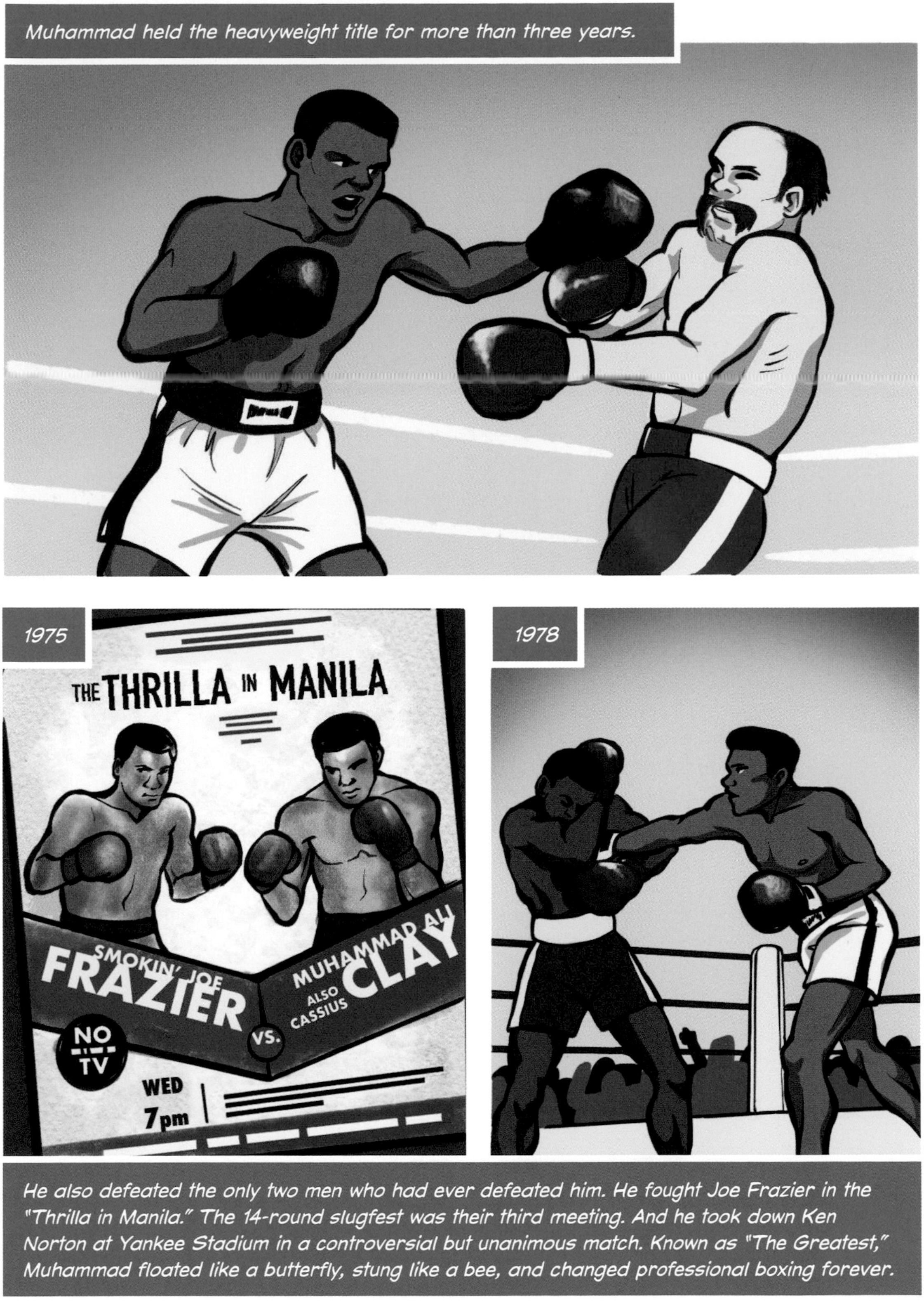
Muhammad held the heavyweight title for more than three years.
1975
THE THRILLA IN MANILA
SMOKIN' JOE FRAZIER
VS.
MUHAMMAD ALI
ALSO CASSIUS CLAY
NO TV
WED 7pm
1978
He also defeated the only two men who had ever defeated him. He fought Joe Frazier in the "Thrilla in Manila." The 14-round slugfest was their third meeting. And he took down Ken Norton at Yankee Stadium in a controversial but unanimous match. Known as "The Greatest," Muhammad floated like a butterfly, stung like a bee, and changed professional boxing forever.

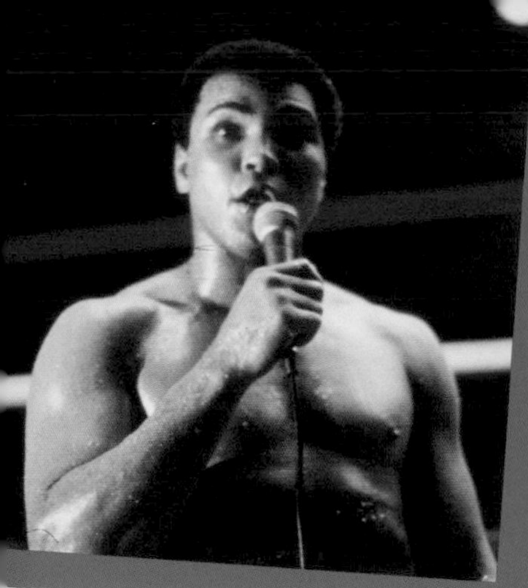

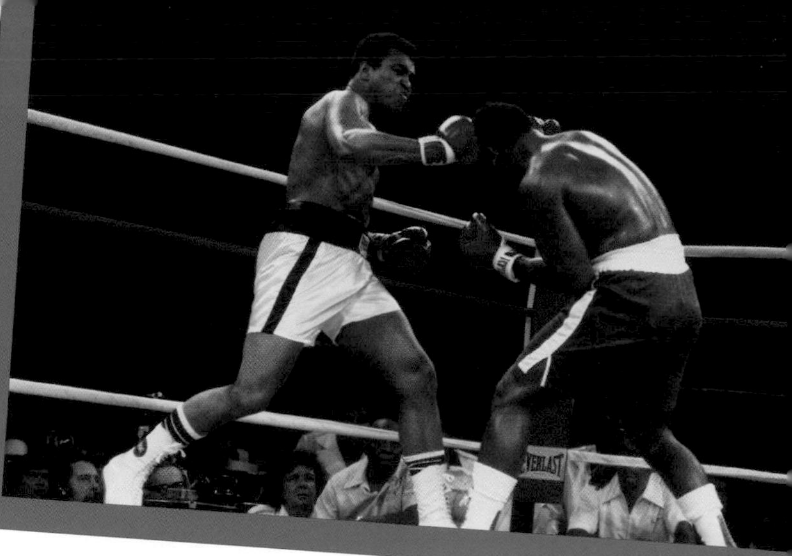

AFTERWORD

Muhammad retired in 1981 with a professional record of 56–5. Many fans consider him to be the G.O.A.T. (Greatest of All Time.)

He focused on humanitarian work after his boxing career. Even after he was diagnosed with Parkinson's disease, he worked to help hungry people around the world. He spoke to people across the United States on the value of education.

His daughter, Laila, followed in her father's footsteps. She won multiple championships. She finished her boxing career undefeated at 24–0.

A replica of Muhammad's stolen red bicycle still hangs above the site of the old Columbia Gym in Louisville, Kentucky.

ATHLETE SNAPSHOT

BIRTH NAME: Cassius Marcellus Clay Jr.

NICKNAMES: The Louisville Lip, The Greatest

BORN: January 17, 1942

DIED: June 3, 2016

Awards of Note

◆ 1960–Olympic gold medalist

◆ 1964, 1974, and 1978–World Heavyweight Champion of the World

◆ 1974–*Sports Illustrated* Sportsperson of the Year

◆ 1990–Boxing Hall of Fame

◆ 2000–*Sports Illustrated* Athlete of the Century

◆ 2005–Presidential Medal of Freedom

◆ 2009–NAACP Image Award

SOURCE NOTES

16   Muhammad Ali. *The Soul of a Butterfly: Reflections on Life's Journey.* New York: Simon & Schuster, 2004.

19   Muhammad Ali, *Twitter*, January 5, 2017 https://twitter.com/muhammadali/status/817151199279509504

19   Tom Goldman, "Boxer Muhammad Ali, 'The Greatest Of All Time,' Dies At 74," *Illinois Public Media*, June 4, 2016, https://will.illinois.edu/news/story/boxer-muhammad-ali-the-greatest-of-all-time-dies-at-74

23   Fred Barbash, "50 Years Ago, Muhammad Ali Was Told to 'Step Forward.' He Refused." *Washington Post*, April 18, 2017, https://www.washingtonpost.com/news/morning-mix/wp/2017/04/28/muhammad-ali-50-years-ago-today-was-told-to-step-forward-he-refused/

GLOSSARY

abolitionist: a person who fought to end slavery

amateur: a person who plays a sport as a hobby

appeal: a request to a higher court to reverse a lower court's decision

Civil Rights Movement: a social and political movement; its goal was to end racial segregation

controversial: something that causes a disagreement

draft: a selection of a person or group for a purpose

jab: a quick, sharp blow

passive resistance: nonviolent opposition to authority

qualify: to earn the right to compete in a certain event or class

segregation: the act of keeping people or groups apart

split decision: a decision made by boxing judges to declare a winner by majority rule

FURTHER INFORMATION

Britannica Kids: Muhammad Ali
https://kids.britannica.com/students/article/Muhammad-Ali/272808

Ducksters: Biography for Kids: Muhammad Ali
https://www.ducksters.com/biography/athletes/muhammad_ali.php

Fishman, Jon M. *Boxing's G.O.A.T.: Muhammad Ali, Manny Pacquiao, and More.* Minneapolis: Lerner Publications, 2022.

Helping Kids Rise: Muhammad Ali
https://www.helpingkidsrise.org/post/2016/06/05/muhammad-ali-for-kids
-the-man-the-legend-the-thinker

Roberts, Randy. *Muhammad Ali and Malcolm X: The Fatal Friendship*. New York: Little, Brown and Company, 2023.

Soria, Gabriel. *Who Was the Greatest?: Muhammad Ali*. New York: Penguin Workshop, 2022.

INDEX